POVERTY ON A SMALL PLANET

POVERTY
ON A SMALL PLANET

A Christian Looks at Living Standards

EDWARD ROGERS

The Macmillan Company
New York

First American Edition 1965

© SCM Press Ltd. 1964

First published in England in 1964 under the title
LIVING STANDARDS
A Christian Looks at World Poverty

Library of Congress Catalog card number: 65-10282

Printed in Great Britain

CONTENTS

PREFACE

WHAT should be the Christian response to the motives and hopes of the campaign to free the world from hunger? The question is not rhetorical, though it may seem so. The denominations, officially, have been enthusiastic and of one mind. Local churches, groups, and individuals have worked with devotion and imagination to aid the poor and hungry. Are they wasting their time in vain effort?

There is no doubt that in the churches, and among men of goodwill generally, the tide of sympathy for the developing nations is flowing strongly. One sign of it is the scrupulous avoidance of terms that might possibly offend the susceptibilities of Africans or Asians. No pleader for an attack on the problem of world poverty ever speaks of 'backward nations'. Even 'under-developed nations' is suspect. The *mot juste* is 'developing'. A more obvious sign is the financial response from the British public. For the first time, both Inter-Church Aid and War on Want raised more than a million pounds in 1963. Ox-Fam, zooming to massive dimensions from a humble beginning, dared confidently to ask for a million pounds in the last three months of the year.

The zeal that once poured into missionary enterprise or the support of local hospitals, now spurs Youth Clubs to buy Tractors for the Hungry, and Women's Institutes to adopt agricultural development schemes on the other side of the world. Young Farmers and university students, churches and Rotary clubs, provide bread and cheese lunches and charge for three-course meals. The grim fact that two-thirds of the world's population are undernourished is driven home by ceaseless reiteration.

Incongruous among the confident exhortations and subtle persuasions to extravagance on the public hoardings and in the advertisement columns of the newspapers, a small child looks out with uncomplaining, haunting eyes; the skeleton at the feast of the affluent society. The motives for response to his appeal are obvious and honourable. 'If a brother or sister be naked, and destitute of daily food, and one of you say unto them, Depart in peace, be ye warmed and filled; notwithstanding ye give them not those things which are needful to the body; what doth it profit?'

There may be a romantic appeal, capturing the imagination, in the very size of the enterprise. There may be an encouraging consolation in the feeling that here is a good cause in which theological and denominational barriers melt away. There may, for some, be an uneasy sense that the wealth of the West was immorally acquired, and that the war against world poverty opens a way for penitent restitution. There may, for others, be a calculation that a widening gap between the poor nations and the rich may endanger the security of the rich, and that narrowing the gap would be sensible insurance. But the basic motive, without question, is simple, uncomplicated compassion.

Is compassion enough? It is not easy to be critical of such enthusiastic benevolence; not easy to pause to examine long-term probabilities under the eyes of the child in the poster. But when so much effort and devotion is being enlisted, it is essential to attempt a realistic appraisal of the enterprise. There are critics of repute who assert that, in order to stimulate generosity, an unbalanced and inaccurate picture is being given of the extent of world poverty and hunger. Facts are often distorted in the stresses of advocacy. In an eloquent Christmas sermon a very well-known preacher wrung the hearts of his hearers by describing the sufferings of the starving two-thirds of the world. He was talking eloquent nonsense—but what are the facts?

Some students of world trends have concluded, sadly, that the whole noble enterprise is hopeless. World population is growing too fast. The rate of aid for developing countries has been steadily accelerating for fifteen years, and things are worse now than then. We are in a *Looking Glass* world, running fast but not quite fast enough even to stay where we are. Every year scientific advance increases productivity, makes land more fertile, and reclaims the desert; but every year there are another fifty million hungry mouths to feed, most of them uttering their first new-born cries where hunger is already most acute. The theoretical solution is obvious enough. Slow down the rate of population increase and step up the rate of productivity increase. But, in the sort of world we have, is this a practical possibility? If not, must we lower our sights?

There are others who tell us that the methods so uncritically adopted are self-defeating. The normal end-product of unconsidered compassion is charity. Perpetual dependence on charity is not simply a buffer against reality. It undermines personal and national initiative, and can make the last state of the recipient community worse than that first state of distress which aroused the external impulse to charity. It may seem callous to leave a suffering nation to be driven to seek its own salvation by the cruel, relentless spurs of economic necessity, but, so it is argued, it will be kinder in the long run than if the will to effort is weakened by hand-outs. Once, and not so very long ago, all the nations of the world were poor. Those now called wealthy gained their prosperity, after painful struggles, by their own enterprise; and those now called poor must follow the same road. This, to the tender heart, is a most unattractive argument—but is there any measure of truth in it?

Another uneasy query comes from a wholly different quarter. Ought Christians to be plunging so gaily into enterprises primarily designed to raise material living standards? The object appears to be to raise Africa and Asia to the level of the United States and Scandinavia, but the quality of life in the affluent nations of the West calls for no resounding hallelujahs. Suicide rates, divorce rates, and delinquency rates climb in parallel with living standards. The pressures and tensions of money-based, industrialized urban society claim a swelling army of victims to mental illness.

Behind the charitably hesitant disquiet looms the blunt question: would it really be for the greater good of the human race to submerge all the five continents under the deadly weight of Subtopia? The common sensual man may want evermore to be building bigger and better barns. The poor may long to be rich, and the rich richer. But ought not Christians to be warning against the vain pursuits of acquisitiveness, and plainly reminding us that a man's life consisteth not in the abundance of his possessions?

Finally, there are some who look sceptically on the optimistic assertion that a general material enrichment will bring nearer the day of peace on earth. Depressingly, they point out that it is when nations wax fat that they begin to kick.

These critical voices are not loud, but they should be heeded. My own view is that they offer guidance in the exercise of compassion. Each takes a valid point and exaggerates it unjustifiably. Our responsibility is to assess the measure of validity and use it as a control. The critics are going against a very strong public opinion, and are liable to be dismissed out of hand as mean-spirited reactionaries, but they may be talking sense. In such an enterprise, a powerful surge in the wrong direction, or ill-led in the right direction, could do incalculable harm.

Because I realize the gravity of that warning I have not, in the pages that follow, started with the statement of a case and then sought to defend it against all objections. I have chosen deliberately to try to be more judicial than homiletical; to take those critical questions entirely seriously and to approach them without presupposing the answers, and then to face the questions that arise out of the provisional answers. Wherever it is possible, I have looked for factual and objective grounds for the answers. I have gathered some unexpected information on the way, and have seen some fixed ideas shatter under the barrage of inconvenient but undeniable facts. But how far I have been unbiassed it is not for me to say. For I came out at the end with no modified and moderated judgement. I began with the inner conviction that an assault on world poverty and hunger was a worthy act of Christian compassion. I ended with a deeper conviction that here is a Christian imperative.

EDWARD ROGERS

March 1964

I

FINDING THE FACTS

POVERTY is a relative condition; a circumstance which makes factual analysis particularly difficult. Oliver Goldsmith's country parson was 'passing rich with forty pounds a year'. The value of money has changed considerably since the village of Auburn was deserted, but even when translated into present purchasing power his stipend was well below the standard now earnestly desired by the Church Commissioners. Yet he was not a poor man. The comparison was with the income of the farm labourers who made up his congregation. By that comparison, which both he and they would accept as normal, he was indeed passing rich.

In *The Other America*, an interesting and informative counter-blast to *The Affluent Society*, Mr Michael Harrington has described the hard lot of the forty or fifty million poor in the United States. The cut-off, the mark below which poverty begins, is taken as an annual income of between $3,000 and $3,500 for an urban family of four, with a hint that this is rather on the mean side and that it ought to be nearer $4,000. To the peasant labourer of Laos or Peru that would be incredible. Half as much would be abundant wealth. But the comparison is with the normal income and normal expectations of the American skilled worker. By that accepted social standard under $3,000 a year is humiliating poverty.

In other words, and it is as well to get this clear right at the beginning, discussion about poverty and living standards is ultimately subjective. In fact, the whole question of the accepted concept of the nature of the good life is involved. The artisan in our own country who demands a living wage (and the Methodist minister who hopes for one), and reckons in that living wage the rent for his television set and his hire purchase payments for a washing machine and a refrigerator, is not being unconsciously selfish and greedy. These are things which are currently accepted in the social setting of the skilled British worker as reasonable and desirable living accessories; and if he cannot afford them he is a poor man.

The standard of the reasonable and desirable is perpetually changing, and we shall have to look more closely at this later. The compulsion which makes much want more is one of the dominant drives of human society. The wings of the acquisitive imagination begin to spread once a man (or woman) is tolerably well fed, well housed, and well clothed. Indeed, once a man or a society has broken free from the shackles of abject need, it appears to be taken for granted that there must be continuous progress to higher and higher living standards.

But surely, it may be argued, when our main concern is with the massive problem of the societies which are still on the rock-bottom of subsistence level this is largely irrelevant. The family that does not know where its next meal is coming from, or if there will be a next meal, is too absorbed in the desperate struggle for survival to worry about keeping up with the Joneses. That is true enough, but even at the levels where the struggle for life is most grim the concept of poverty is relative and subjective.

One of the reasons why a problem that is as old as mankind has suddenly burst upon us with shocking force is that the area of comparison has widened. When a peasant drudged from dawn till dark to win a scanty harvest from thin soil, as all his neighbours did, and as his father and grandfather had done before him, and as his children and grandchildren would do after him, he would know that life was hard and might wonder why God made it so. But knowing that such was the pattern of life in his village and all the villages nearby and presumably, therefore, of all the world, he would not regard himself as poor unless through illness or drought he became starving and destitute.

Awareness of what the rest of the world really looks like, or rather of what it looks like on the cinema screen and sounds like on the radio, has brought swiftly in its train awareness of poverty. The miracle of modern communications has shrunk the world for the diplomat, the business man, and the soldier. The ecclesiastical top brass glide smoothly from Delhi to Geneva, to Toronto to Accra. And in a bush clearing an Asian peasant sees the solid prosperity of small-town America flickering hazily on a silver screen. He sees the cars, the sidewalks, the drugstores, the electric lights, the bathrooms . . . and discovers that he is poor. As H. J. P. Arnold comments at the beginning of his valuable study, *Aid for Developing Countries*, behind the turbulence of the confused revolutions of the twentieth century lies 'the revolution of rising expectations'.

Yet, oddly enough, it was the attempt to elucidate and apply objective standards that brought awareness to the more comfortable countries of the poverty of others. Travellers observed the happy, carefree, unsophisticated natives, praising the persistence among them of the stalwart virtues that were fast disappearing in the money-making West. The romanticization of tribal loyalties and exotic customs, of the sort that still pops up occasionally in reminiscent articles in *The Times*, took no account of calories and proteins. Nutritional scientists like Hopkins and Dr John Boyd Orr (as he then was) talked of such mysteries thirty years ago, adding to them the deeper mysteries of enzymes and proteins and trace elements. So long as they stuck to pure science or to animal nutrition they were listened to with puzzled respect. But when they applied their science to human beings in the bleak years of the Depression between the World Wars there was trouble.

They organized Committees Against Malnutrition. They assessed the nutritive value of the diets of school children and miners. Boyd Orr wrote *Food, Health and Income*. The estimate that half the population of Britain was inadequately fed was ridiculed as gross exaggeration, explained away by reference to the incompetence of British housewives or stolidly ignored. But that survey of thirty years ago has led directly to the Freedom from Hunger campaign. It provided an objective, scientific standard by which to measure hunger, and so, by a simple extension, to measure poverty.

In the intervening thirty years a cascade of statistics has poured forth; on calorie intake per person per annum, on the average expectation of life, on infant mortality, on *per capita* income. It gives a deceptive impression of precision. The fact has to be faced that in many countries, and especially in those for which the figures are most depressing, there are no facilities for gathering accurate statistical information. For the greater part of Asia, Africa, and Latin America the solid-seeming figures are estimates. According to the subject and the country, the margin of error can swing from ten to as high as fifty per cent. It will be remembered, for example, that in the autumn of 1963 there was a complicated political row in Nigeria about the census. The political issues are irrelevant for our purposes, but the point is that as this is being written there is no reliable figure for the population of Nigeria. It follows logically that there can be no accurate figure, even if all the rest of the evidence was available, for infant mortality per thousand of population or for average income per head.

Lack of adequate evidence is not the only reason for warning that statistical tables should be observed with a wary eye. The non-scientist is apt to disregard the reservations and conditional clauses of the scientist. The most clinically impersonal and scientific attempt to provide a norm for the measurement of hunger considers the human body as a machine that needs an adequate supply of fuel if it is to function effectively. The approach is perfectly legitimate. The conclusion of the physiological and nutritional experts of the Food and Agriculture Organization is that for such effective functioning a man needs to take in one calorie per hour for every kilogramme of his weight. The calorific value of various foodstuffs can be calculated precisely. From all the calculations emerges the estimate that to keep him functioning effectively a man's diet should provide him with a daily intake of 2,500 calories.

This looks to be, and has been taken to be, the magnificent simplicity we need. All we have to do is to draw a dividing line at the 2,500 level. Those below the mark are inadequately nourished. Those on or above it are adequately fed. But this is to ignore the abstract averageness of the standard. It has to be adjusted to age, occupation and climate. The young need proportionately more calories than the old. The sedentary worker needs less than the manual worker. The basis for the estimate is an average temperature of fifteen degrees Centigrade, and as the temperature rises the quantity of essential calorific intake falls. A large young Eskimo sealer ought to have more than 3,000, and an Ituri pygmy clerk, if there is such a creature, could get by comfortably on 2,000.

Moreover, though it is a reasonable assumption for this particular purpose that the human body can be considered as a machine, it is a peculiarly complicated machine. Calories are not enough. An ample and unvaried diet of large slabs of suet pudding would stuff with calories to bursting point the frame of the unfortunate consumer, but it would not adequately nourish him. The body is a complex of co-operating mechanisms, and each has its own need. A fully balanced diet should include varying proportions of twelve different vitamins, traces of several mineral salts, and proteins which should provide fourteen distinct and non-interchangeable amino-acids.

What this means is that there is neither enough reliable evidence nor a sufficiently simple standard test to enable us to determine with meticulous precision the extent of world hunger. The same cautious proviso has to be made about the monetary measurement of world poverty. Those tables which neatly range the nations of the world in descending order of average income per head expressed in United States dollars have little of the sadly inevitable accuracy of our personal bank balances. As we have already observed, where the need is greatest, the reliable statistics are fewest. The method exaggerates the disparity between the rich nations and the poor, for the richer a nation is the more completely its economy is monetary. Peasant communities exchange by barter goods that Americans buy in supermarkets. Services are performed in family and kinship circles without charge for which the industrial worker has to pay. The more the tertiary services expand in an economy —and in the wealthier nations they are expanding fast—the more money income goes in transactions that never appear in simpler economies. The Bolivian peasant rarely has to worry about car insurance, school uniforms, television licences, and cloakroom tips. It is a simple enough matter to translate rupees into dollars at the current rate of exchange, but a straightforward comparison of average incomes so calculated does not give a fair picture of the contrast between the wealth of Utah and the poverty of Uttar Pradesh.

But the fact that poverty and hunger cannot be measured with a scientific precision comparable to that with which the tensile strength of a steel bar can be measured does not sweep the whole appalling problem out of sight. It means that preachers and speakers who stand as advocates for the hungry must learn to handle percentages and statistical tables with care, recognizing that they are provisional estimates. Those who have so laboriously compiled the estimates do not need the caution. They know only too well that no more than the foundation of their work is ascertained fact. Most of the filling in is a mixture of incomplete fact and intelligent deduction, and occasional gaps have still, for the time being, to be covered by reasonable guesswork. Their scientific integrity is outraged by well-intentioned emotional appeals on behalf of the 'starving two-thirds of the human race'.

(It is, in passing, just as well that this too frequent tear-jerker is wrong. If it were really true that two thousand million human beings were starving, we should have to admit that the problem was beyond any mortal solution.)

All that the experts of United Nations claim to have done has been to give us a reasonably fair assessment of the actual situation. Their claim stands up to examination. Within the limits set by the imprecise nature of their evidence they have used objective standards to map in rough outline the dominion of poverty and hunger. The imprecision does not weaken the impact of their judgements. Nor does it sustain the critics who argue that the whole thing has been grossly exaggerated.

One has a reluctant sympathy with these critics. They wonder how it is that the problem of world poverty has so suddenly zoomed to such vast proportions, and suspect that most of it has been created by clever men playing around with statistics. They are made uneasy by the obvious exaggeration of some popular advocacy. They are only half convinced that the rapidly accelerating rise in world population is a sufficient answer. What they do not realize is that, basically, they are falling into the same error as the over-zealous whom they criticize.

The less important part of the answer to their doubts has already been given. The hunger is not new. The problem is new because new means of communication have made the world more aware of itself and made the poor aware of their poverty. Global social surveys have dug beneath the surface seen by the tourist and the business traveller. But the most important part of the answer is that nutritional science is beginning to educate us to understand the real nature of hunger. The clue is in the catalogue of calories and amino-acids, vitamins and trace elements. The problem is not mainly one of starvation. That grimly provides its own solution. It is the problem of concealed hunger, of the under-nourishment that lets a man live but that handicaps and cripples his living.

Starvation is the child of destitution. Concealed hunger is the child of poverty. The map drawn by the experts is for the most part a map of such hunger—and the most optimistic reading of it is profoundly disturbing. It is a new map because the science of nutrition is a new science; a record of the discovery of something that has always been with us, and not the insubstantial fabrication of a statistician.

In *The Challenge of Hunger* Father Noel Drogat has drawn an actual map of calorie intake. When all the qualifications and provisos are remembered, they do not blur the clear message. The daily supply in the United States, Argentina, Britain, Scandinavia, Australia and New Zealand is over 3,000. Canada, the Soviet Union, and Western Europe have between 2,600 and 3,000. Central America, Brazil, West Africa, South Africa, Egypt and Central Europe have between 2,200 and 2,600. The rest, including most of Africa and all of Asia, have less than 2,200

All the other related figures conform to this geography. The infant mortality rate for every thousand live births is 23 in New Zealand, 25 in the United Kingdom, 48 in Italy, 113 in India. The average expectation of life from the day of birth is 70 years in the United States, 67 in the Soviet Union, 53 in Brazil, and 32 in India. Paul Hoffman's elaborate calculation of annual income per head, based on the figures from 1957 to 1959, lists no less than 52 countries and territories where it falls below one hundred dollars. With the single exception of Albania, all are in Asia, Africa, the Arab lands, the West Indies, and South America. There are another thirty where it is under two hundred dollars, but there is still no European nation to be added. Britain comes in at the 800 mark, Switzerland at 850, Canada at 870, the United States at 1,500.

The love of statistics is an acquired taste, and not one

widely acquired, so few have been given. But their import is inescapable. It is a fact that the majority of mankind is poor and hungry. It is a fact that we now know it is a fact. The times of our ignorance God winked at, but now we are called to action.

2

TO HIM THAT HATH

ONE of the hardest sayings in all the gospels comes in the the parable of the Talents. In the Gospel according to St Matthew it reads: 'For unto every one that hath shall be given, and he shall have abundance; but from him that hath not, even that which he hath shall be taken away.'

The temptation to expound the theological significance of the comment must be resisted. The point to note here is that it is founded on an accurate observation of a reality of human existence. It is a fact that power attracts power and money breeds money. I am informed, though I cannot as yet vouch for the truth of the information, that the toughest patch for an aspiring millionaire is the collection of his first hundred thousand pounds. Once he has got so far he has a steady interest income, he has the right sort of contacts, and he has a safe reserve out of which to take potentially profitable risks. If he keeps his head down and is prepared to think more about his business than about wintering in sunny indolence in the Bahamas, the rest is fairly easy.

Such opulent advice has its own peculiar charm, but is not much help to the man who is down to his last half-crown, or even to the young couple with a growing family and a heavily mortgaged house. It may seem unjust that the prospects are worst for those whose needs are greatest, but that is how it is. The typist has a luncheon voucher, the managing director an expense account. A top-ranking star in the world of entertainment can pick and choose from a varied selection of remunerative engagements, and can in addition do very well from the extras attracted by his fame, endorsing cigarettes or hair cream, appearing for a consideration at garden parties and association dinners, writing —or signing—articles on Modern Youth, Religion, or the Eschatological Significance of the Second Law of Thermodynamics. The old trouper who never quite made the grade grows slowly more seedy as he waits with diminishing hope for his one lucky break.

Where competition is really fierce, as, in the world of business, between daily newspapers or stores or betting shops, the strong get stronger and the weak get weaker. The same built-in pressure to widening disparity operates in the relationship of nations. There is, fortunately, a compensatory resistance. If life in all its aspects was a merciless struggle for survival, with no holds barred, the weak and the handicapped would inevitably perish. The operations of compassion and charity, of love within the family, kindly tradition within the tribe, and welfare services within the nation, blunt the sharp edges of the sword of social conflict. But though the bitterness of the struggle is modified, it is not abolished. Unless there is compassion and charity, the weak go to the wall.

It is not, therefore, wholly realistic to argue that the poorer nations must better their condition by their own unaided efforts. They must take the main responsibility, but they need a helping hand. There was a time, and not very long ago in the whole span of human history, when all the nations were in more or less the same position. A dominating military aristocracy, served by a small and moderately affluent merchant group, ruled over a peasant community. When every nation was at about the same low level, it was possible for some to rise by their own initiative.

The fortunate mixing of such ingredients as national homogeneity and political stability, climatic conditions neither too relaxing nor too severe, intellectual awakening and the development of scientific skills, and the possession of easily accessible raw materials, provided the fuel for a take-off. Once the pressure was well under way the rate of acceleration speeded. Those who insist that, in the contemporary situation, every nation must still rise wholly by its own efforts, ignore reality. The nations which started early are progressing so fast, and accumulating resources at such an increasing rate, that those which start now can never hope to catch up—unless they are given a boost.

To get this out of the cloudy realm of generalization, let us look, for example, at our own country. Ever since the national pride of Britain was outraged by President de Gaulle's brusque refusal to let us into the Common Market, the functioning of our social, economic, and political system has been relentlessly and interminably analysed. (It made little difference to the analysts whether they were in favour of our entry or not. The intolerable thing was to be rejected.) Harrowing pictures have been painted of our slow, deplorable decline. Our share of the world market is shrinking. Our once justly famed products are shoddy. The equipment of our factories is thirty years out of date, and the fixed ideas of both management and unions sixty years out of date. We try to live by the slapdash, casual code of the amateur in a world of slick professionals. With our eyes firmly fixed on the past we hold as an ideal a romanticized concept of the life and virtues of the landed gentry, encouraged to do so by the dominating and paralysing authority of Oxford and Cambridge.

The deliberately doleful analyses make the sort of reading the British enjoy most. They are the pained strictures by the masters of a pupil who could be top of the form if only he would bestir himself—and the pupil is duly flattered. The absurdities of demarcation disputes and the stranglehold of the old boy network are, we complacently reflect, the temporary failings of a people intended by the Almighty to show the rest of mankind how things ought to be done.

As things turned out, the analysts chose a bad time for publication. They wrote to chart a way forward in the first reaction to the Common Market fiasco, in an unprecedently bitter winter when the total number of unemployed was soaring and the pound was wobbling. By the time their efforts reached the bookshops exports were rising to record levels, the rate of industrial productivity remarkably increasing, the total of the unemployed falling, and the pound stronger than for years past. It was also clearly evident that the remedies they proposed precisely echoed the presuppositions and prejudices of the analysts.

But if their gloomiest predictions had been fulfilled, and if their logic had been impartially impeccable, all their suggestions would still be practicable. An enlargement and up-grading of Colleges of Advanced Technology, the creation of specialized institutions for the training of professional managers, colossal expenditure on secondary education, research projects on the application of scientific technology, much greater use of automation in office administration, large capital expenditure on modernizing factory equipment, doubling the available places in the universities—it could all be done if the nation felt like doing it. It would be a strain. Peripheral projects, and comfortable luxuries might have to be deferred, and the order of economic priorities re-shuffled, but the plans are not pipe dreams. After two centuries of industrial development Britain has enough capital resources and technical knowledge to take the strain. To him that hath shall be given. We have enough scholars, scientists, craftsmen, electronics engineers, accountants, architects and the rest to spare some to train more.

Contrast this with the situation in a typical North Indian village. Its people have the inherited, inadequate skills of peasants and manual craftsmen. They depend wholly on the poor crops raised from parched and devitalized soil. At the entrance to the village is a great dump of cow-pats, drying in the sun; later to be used as fuel for cooking. The ten year old son of an English farmer could see at once that, if only the manure were fed into the land, the harvest would be vastly more abundant and the whole village lifted above its level of precarious subsistence. But the ten year old son of an Indian peasant can see it just as clearly. The problem is that they cannot afford to do what they know they ought to do. They have to use something for fuel. They have no money to spare to buy oil. They have no money to spare because there is not enough cash surplus from their crops. There is no cash surplus because the crops are barely enough to keep them alive. The crops are poor because the soil is not nourished. The land is starved because the manure is burned for fuel. The manure is burned because they have no money to spare for oil. And so the vicious circle spins, enfolding them in inescapable poverty. After many centuries of toil and penury, there are no capital resources and no reservoir of trained technological skill to break the circle.

It is tighter than an iron economic grip. Poverty breeds illness. The camp-followers of inadequate or monotonous diet and of rudimentary sanitary conditions, are goitre, scurvy, typhoid fever, pellagra, worm-infestation, dysentery, tuberculosis, blindness, anaemia, and a score of other diseases. They bring lassitude of mind and feebleness of body. Behind the cold statistics of calorie intake and low annual *per capita* income is the reality of sick men guiding primitive ploughs over stony land.

Kwashiorkor, malignant malnutrition, is the scourge of Africa. The word is Bantu, meaning 'red child', for after weaning the victim of this killer disease becomes pot-bellied and comatose, and his hair grows thin and red. He is the child of the posters. There is a simple cure—milk. But, as Noel Drogat observes, milk cannot be produced in sufficient quantities in Africa, and for a long time to come condensed or powdered milk will be beyond the purchasing power of the mass of the people.

Beriberi is the scourge of the rice-eating peoples of Asia. Attributed by the sufferers to an evil spirit which nibbles away the soul—which gives a vivid picture of its course—it is caused by enforced reliance on cheap milled rice as the staple food. The Food and Agricultural Organization Nutrition Committee has made useful suggestions for combating the disease by encouraging the use of rice enriched by comparatively cheap thiamine derivatives, but they know that the best solution is a more varied, and therefore more expensive, diet. Always we come back to the empty hands of the man who hath not; to the realization that if only there was a margin above the bare level of subsistence a way of release could be found—and that there is no margin.

Man is an amazingly adaptable creature. Human communities can survive in the icy wastes of the Arctic, in the fever-laden miasma of the Amazonian jungles, or in the brazen heat of the Sahara. However ill-fed and desperately poor they are, human communities can survive, provided that they can avoid starvation. They adapt to their environment; heat, cold, fever, or poverty. A high birth-rate, at least equalling the high death-rate, ensures survival. Even though one child in three dies before it is a year old, and half die before they reach the age of five, and most of the rest perish prematurely old before they are forty, if enough children are born, the group continues.

The will to live, and to hope, is strong. The irrepressible human spirit will soften and adorn the blackness of the most miserable situation, with customs and traditions, with rites and ceremonies, with magic or superstition, or religion. There is always a place for love and laughter—in spite of the poverty, not because of it. The parents of an infant smitten by beriberi, or of a youth wasted away by tuberculosis, may stoically resign themselves to the inscrutable will of the Great Spirit, or to the inexplicable hostility of a wandering demon, but they do not rejoice to lose their child.

The have-nots of this world must learn to endure. They have little resistance to disease. They are illiterate. But they are not idiots. If they could escape the bondage of the vicious circle, they would.

But is it really true that they cannot? Some of those who insist that every community must lift itself by its own endeavours would be prepared to argue that brooding on dying children and bereaved parents warps the judgement and obscures the way of release in a cloud of sentimentality. There is evidence staring us in the face, they say, that it can be done. In the lifetime of many of us it has been done. The second greatest Power in the world today was not so long ago a nation of backward and primitive peasants. The determined leaders of the Soviet revolution lashed and drove their people out of their backwardness. Men and women who had next to nothing were compelled to accept yet greater hardship and deprivation for the sake of a planned future prosperity. It was agony, but it succeeded. We of the soft-hearted and soft-living West may recoil from the prospect of misery being made still more miserable in order that tomorrow may be bright, though that may be because we forget the more protracted misery of our own industrial revolutions. May it not be that only the shock of a planned and disciplined upheaval can relax the paralysing grip of age-long and fatalistic despair?

An argument like this, normally put much less crudely and with the sharp edges of agony discreetly smoothed away, represents one of the greatest propaganda successes of the Communist apologists. Pre-revolutionary Russia was without question a backward nation. Three-quarters of the working population were illiterate peasants, practising a primitive agriculture and scratching out a subsistence living. But well before 1917 a substantial and expanding industrial sector had been established. Prokopovich, a careful student of Russian economic history, estimates that in 1913 the level of 'national saving', i.e. capital gain available for investment, was as high as ten per cent. When India and China began their Five Year Plans they were still below the level attained in the last days of Tsarist Russia. Olaf Hoeffding has succinctly stated the unfamiliar truth: 'The communists already had the boots and the straps to pull on, whereas contemporary Asia is, relatively speaking, still bare-footed.'

There is, then, not much doubt that if the unprivileged and hungry are to be moved beyond the sticking point of bare existence to the place from which they can go on with hope to a reasonable standard of living, they must be helped on the way; not necessarily carried, but certainly helped.

3

A SMALL PLANET

THE exploits of the astronauts grip the contemporary imagination. They are the supremely dramatic and daring demonstrations of the marvels of science. But they have also a less obvious and possibly more important consequence. They are changing man's attitude to the world on which he lives. When human beings can put a girdle round the earth in less than ninety minutes, and quite confidently expect before long to outstrip the airy speed of Shakespeare's Puck, even though it is extremely difficult for us to grasp the reality and the implications of the achievement, it brings disturbingly to us dawning awareness that we inhabit a comparatively small planet.

In the preceding chapters we have sketched briefly the plight of many of our fellows. The hearts and consciences of Christians, and indeed of all men of goodwill, are stirred by the story of their need; but with the impulse of generous sympathy is mingled a new and sombre note of doubt. In place of the vague vastness of an inexhaustible world we sense the finite, limiting circle of the globe. We may earnestly desire that all should live well—but we may wonder if, after all, this small planet can possibly provide enough to eat for all the teeming multitudes of men.

We can, at least, say quite firmly that the earth is not providing enough at present to feed adequately the whole present human population. This is no more than a preliminary point, but it is worth staying with for a little to clear out of our way a prevalent and dangerous misconception. When we read in the same world as that in which so many go hungry, of the bulging granaries of Canada and

the United States, of potential harvests deliberately re-
tricted by quotas, of coffee burned and fish ground into
fertilizer and milk poured in thousands of gallons down the
drain, it seems that there is a simple, drastic solution to
the problem. Let us take the surplus food from the countries
that have so much more than they need and give it to those
which have so little. If the obstacles to such just redistribu-
tion are the short-sighted folly of politicians, the greed of
farmers and merchants, and the wicked strangling web of
the financiers, then we must fight to overthrow these evils
for the sake of common welfare.

The reaction is as simple and as dangerously half true as
the idea that soaking the rich will relieve all the burdens
of the poor. Something on these lines can be done. In
point of fact, a considerable quantity of surplus foodstuff is
so transferred through various agencies of the United
Nations. But it has to be done with great circumspection,
and within closely defined limits, not because of the callous
indifference of the bountifully supplied nations—who would
be rather pleased to be rid of their unwanted excess—but
because the governments of the needy nations, apart from
their aversion to charity, know quite well that large-scale
dumping would utterly destroy their already precarious
economies.

On top of this comes the further complication of human
idiosyncracy. Those bulging Canadian granaries are full of
wheat, not of rice; and the traditional rice-eater takes a
great deal of persuading that flour is the basis of excellent
and nutritious food. The world problem could be immeasur-
ably reduced if Hindus and Moslems could be convinced that pork is a meat fit to be eaten by properly pious
humans.

But even if we could transfer every scrap of surplus
without injurious effects, could diminish the over-eating of
the affluent to increase the surplus, and could overcome the
repugnancies and taboos, there would still not be enough to
feed adequately every human being. The fact that the

burden of the world's hunger cannot be lifted by a bold, dramatic gesture does not, of course, mean that what can be done is a waste of time and effort. Renewed vigour and revived hope are being given to thousands by the operations of the UN agencies, and of Church World Service and similar voluntary agencies. We know that it relieves but a tiny fraction of the distress, but we know also that a little is better than nothing. All the social services of the Church, whatever their sphere of activity, have come to terms with the fact that for every one they help a hundred are left unhelped. A score of alcoholics, and a hundred discharged recidivist prisoners, are cared for and won back to self-respect, and every one restored is a triumph, not made less because straitened resources prevent the extension of the service. This is as true against the massive evil of world poverty as against this familiar smaller scale.

The cry of every devoted social worker is that he could do so much more that needs doing if only he had greater resources at his disposal. Without them, he lowers his sights and accepts the inevitable limitation. The question, as we consider world poverty and hunger, is whether or not the necessary resources can ever be made available. If not, we should limit our ambitions to the attainable, and not create yet greater tragedy by rousing vain hopes in those we long to aid. The world does not now feed all its people adequately. Could it do so, even if we brought to bear greater wisdom, greater charity, greater skill, and greater determination?

The fundamental question is easier to ask than to answer. Basically, the answer depends upon the amount of land on the planet that can be cultivated, the efficiency of the cultivation, and the total number of people to be fed, but all the factors are inter-related and changing. Just about the only permanent fact is that the surface area of the world amounts to just under two hundred million square miles, or 126,000,000,000 acres. Estimates of the total land area vary within a range of a hundred acres—which is quite a lot of room to play with—but somewhere around 34,000,000,000 acres would be a fair average.

This includes, of course, such places as the arid deserts, the peak of Everest, and the frozen wastes of polar Antarctica; but between the fertile fields of Kent and the dead land of the Kalahari desert there are many gradations of actual and potential fertility. At present roughly 3,000 million acres are under arable cultivation, 3,600 million used for pasture, and 5,700 million occupied for cultivated or natural forest.

It is possible to extend the productive area. The rich farmlands of the English Fen country have been wrested from the embrace of the sea. The brilliant engineering of the Dutch is continually and peaceably pushing outward the frontiers of Holland. Much of the earth's desert is man-made. At last the centuries-long process of short-sighted and ignorant devastation is being halted and reversed. The amount of 'new land' that could be won is fractional, but is not negligible. A half of one per cent of 34,000 million acres can grow a great deal of food.

But there is another, and a much more impressive, method of expansion. Sixty years ago, for example, the quantity of potential wheat-growing land was apparently eternally fixed by rainfall and temperature. A moderate climate and at least eighteen inches of rainfall a year were essential. The geneticists have bred a hardier wheat, shorter, heavier, and less leafy. The acreage under wheat in Canada has swept from four million to thirty million within a generation, and the Australian acreage has trebled. Like an advancing sea as the tide rises the line of fertility is being pushed into the sub-Arctic and the arid lands.

If water can be diverted or discovered, yet more immense areas can be added. Control of the turbulent, side-swiping rivers of Asia and Africa would free wide margins of permanently fertile land along the river banks, and irrigation systems made more practicable by such control could bring life-giving water to the dead soil of the hinterlands. By the

B

skilful use of water Israel is making the desert of the Negev blossom like a rose. In *Common Sense about a Starving World*—a very good book with a very bad title—Ritchie Calder describes the recent discovery of an underground sea of fresh water in the middle of the Sahara, beneath an area of potentially fertile land the size of Great Britain. It is a 'nodular sandstone aquifer in the Intercalary Continental Formation'. Above it is soil, dried out for centuries, which has been preserved and protected by a thin layer of gravel. Since 1960, by a careful pumping out of water in quantities that do not exceed the annual inflow into the vast subterraneous reservoir, trees and crops have thrived where none has been seen for millennia. The grim, forbidding Tanezrouft has slept through the ages, waiting for the reviving kiss of water.

If to all this is added the land that could be restored to use by the eradication of the tsetse fly, and by the draining of swamps, it is encouragingly clear that the garden of Earth could be greatly enlarged. By how much is a matter for conjecture. Some experts estimate that the cultivable area could be doubled. And if this seems to be wildly over-optimistic it may be noted that scientific development has progressively made more ridiculous every cautiously pessimistic prediction.

The second factor of the equation on which the prospects of the human race depend is agricultural efficiency. On the whole, man's record is pretty poor. He has stupidly, and to his own hurt, looted and ravaged the planet. Greedily and ignorantly upsetting the delicate precision of the balance of Nature, he has chopped down and burned trees that guarded and held the soil. He has descended on the savannahs and the prairies, squandered their wealth of fertility with reckless prodigality, and left in his trail a desert or a dust-bowl. After the years of careless ease come the centuries of unrewarding toil.

Fortunately, the record is not wholly one of myopic folly. There are fields in China that still yield bountifully after four thousand years of cropping. There are English farms recorded in the Domesday Book that are far more fertile now than they were nine centuries ago. The art and science of agriculture, which is the application of an intelligence that thinks of tomorrow as well as today, quite literally yields rich and continuing harvests. As Mr. Krushchev has somewhat belatedly realized, the land must be fed if it is to be kept in good heart. His decision to spend less on ballistic missiles and more on fertilizers is a recognition of this fundamental fact.

There is, fortunately, no need to try to summarize a manual of modern agriculture in order to deal adequately with the second factor. The most city-bred Briton, commuting daily from a flat without a garden to a glass and concrete office, has some awareness of the revolution in British farming. The suburban gardener, pottering about happily with selective weed-killers, DDT sprays, new strains of seed, and a garden shed bulging with chemicals in tins and tubes and sacks, is well aware of it. The knowledge and resources are now available to double the yield even of good land which has been well farmed. But nearly three quarters of the farming families of the world are scratching around with primitive ploughs and mattocks just as their remote ancestors were. If all the land now under some form of cultivation was properly fed, sown with good seed, and farmed with full efficiency, supplies would far outpass what is now gathered. If all the land that could be under cultivation was so husbanded, the deadly threat of world hunger would be vastly weakened.

Some deduction must be made for the land in productive use that is not producing food, either directly as edible crops or indirectly as pasture for animals. A sizable acreage is occupied by cultivated forest, supplying timber and, to an increasing extent, pulp for paper. Crops like cotton and flax take up a fair amount of room. So does tobacco. An increased population, and even more a higher living standard, would inevitably claim for a time an additional share of land. It need not, however, be a permanently expanding claim. Skilled arboriculture gets better returns each decade from smaller areas. Synthetic fibres provide more and more clothing material. And the combined efforts of the Royal College of Physicians and the Surgeon General of the United States may yet diminish the demand for cigarettes.

A tiny shadow of doubt dims the brightness of this prospect. Everyone who writes about potential food production mentions Sir William Crookes. Some point out how foolish he was to argue that shortage of nitrate fertilizers would inevitably halt the progress of agriculture. Others praise his wisdom in asserting that the thing most needful was to develop an abundant supply of nitrates. All agree that if heavy crops are taken out of the soil, fertilizers have to be put back. As we can now get nitrogen from the air there is not likely to be a shortage for very many years to come.

It is just as well. The United States is producing and consuming over three million tons a year. According to Dr Baade, an eminent agricultural scientist and head of the Research Institute for Economic Problems of Developing Countries at Bonn, sugar-beet growers in Western Europe are using 220 lbs per hectare (2·5 acres). Pastures in Holland are given 330 lb per hectare annually. The average for all types of land in Japan is 220 lb per hectare. Incidentally, in *The Race to the Year 2000* Dr Baade draws a map to illustrate the world use of plant nutrients. It was devised entirely independently, but it could be taken as a photostat of Father Drogat's map of levels of calorific intake.

The faintly disturbing question mark is not about the supply of nitrates and phosphates and selective chemicals. It is about their long-term effects. Man has been pumping these inorganic quickeners into his land for not much more than a single human generation. Will the land continue to respond? Or will the graph of productivity pass its peak and begin to fall as the concentrated chemical forcing enervates the soil? The chemists tell us that we have no cause to worry—but here and there voices are raised, not obscurantist or reactionary, to warn us that Nature must be handled gently and slowly. It is conceivable that the cycle of life may be distorted by overdoses of the inorganic.

Supposing, however, that all goes well, that new land is found, old land improved, efficient husbandry practised, and the confidence of the scientists justified; there is still another problem. Will there be enough water? The problem is so rarely raised by the experts that it may not be a genuine problem, though there have been disquieting comments from the United States that water is being used faster than it is being replaced by rainfall. The dog-fight in Palestine about the headwaters of the Jordan is primarily a political-military attempt by the Arab States to put the squeeze on Israel, but it reflects also a concern about the commodity which is as important as land itself. It has been forcefully argued that a lowering of the water table, which would incidentally drain swamps and marshes, would be generally beneficial, and that if an intelligent balance were kept there would be no cause for alarm. But it is in keeping an intelligent balance that trouble may arise. I must confess that the technicalities of a difficult subject on which too little research has been done are beyond me, but it is an interesting speculation that the world-wide extension of America's plumbing may not be compatible with an adequate world food supply.

It is a possibility that the pursuit of better living standards may lead to a chronic and frustrating water shortage. It is a fact that the same pursuit swallows up land. Roads, factories, airports, schools, hospitals, libraries, football fields, and office blocks have all to be put somewhere. Growth of population means the growth of towns and cities, devouring farms and pastures as they grow. At the time of the first World War there were only twenty cities with a population that exceeded a million. Now there are more than eighty. I am living in a suburb of ten thousand people that thirty years ago was a village. I moved to it from an ancient hamlet surrounded by new housing estates. In my first appointment, elderly residents of West Ham, living in an endless maze of bricks and mortar, told me of the vanished country lanes of their childhood. Every year in every continent, thousands of acres pass from the farmer to the builder.

This creates additional difficulties about the transport and marketing of food, but, set in the context of total land area, it does not yet present a serious problem. The warnings and hesitations have been listed as a cautious warning against unjustified optimism, but when the most has been made of them it is still obvious that a quite dramatic filling of the world's larder is a practical possibility. In fact, what may appear to be rosy optimism is a serious underestimate. Whenever man thinks of food production he comes in the end to measuring and assessing land. It is time that he brought the same calculating eye to bear on the ninety thousand million acres of sea. One of the great turning points in human history came when nomadic hunters began to settle down and cultivate. Man still hunts, crudely and primitively, the food he gathers from the oceans. His catch-as-catch-can techniques are like those of the land hunters who decimated game or of the ignorant cultivators who turned good soil into desert. Fortunately the damage he has done has been limited by the vastness of the seas and by the inefficiency of his methods.

If he began seriously to farm the seas, instead of plundering, he would step over the threshold of a second nutritional revolution. Even as things now are, almost the whole of the fish marketed is caught in the Northern Hemisphere. The proportion in the Southern Hemisphere, where the need is greatest, barely reaches two per cent of the total. There is, or was, a good reason for this disparity. The really good fishing grounds in the Southern Hemisphere are far from the ports, and fish is a perishable commodity—as well as one that gives unmistakable evidence when it begins to perish. Packing a catch in ice preserves it for a few days only, so that a round trip can extend no further than can be sailed and trawled in twelve to fourteen days. But the limitation has now disappeared. Instant deep-freezing preserves the fish for months, and in a much better condition than natural ice.

The Russian fishing industry made the first experiments with the new techniques. Britain and Norway followed more cautiously. A large factory ship, which is in fact a floating deep-freeze plant, is supplied by a fleet of satellite trawlers. The initial capital cost is high, but the returns are good. There is no reason—except for that high capital cost—why it should not work successfully in the southern latitudes. The most modest estimate I have seen is that it would double the supply and still keep well within the replacement rate of the breeding grounds.

But this is scientific hunting; the pack rather than the lone stalker. In the last decade the scientific farmer has appeared. The monks had their own carp for centuries. The angling clubs mollified the irate floggers of over-fished rivers by breeding their own trout. Why not breed sea fish? I remember reading a few years ago a science-fiction novel by Arthur C. Clarke, depicting under-water shoals grazing on cultivated plankton, guarded and chivvied by the sheep-dogs of the deep—specially trained sharks! It could have been dismissed as a farrago of far-fetched nonsense, except that in earlier novels Mr Clarke had described in similar detail an orbiting communication satellite and a rocket to the moon programme, when these were regarded as flights of imagination also.

A prophet is not a fortune-teller. He is a man clear-eyed enough to see the significant things that are happening around him and intelligent enough to deduce logically from them. In this sense, Mr Clarke was a sound prophet. Experiments have been carried out at the marine research station at Millport. The results, noted in M. Guerrin's *Humanité et subsistances*, are quoted by Father Drogat on p. 104 of

The Conquest of Hunger. '650 pounds of nitrates and 250 pounds of superphosphates were poured into three acres of water. The stimulus given to the plankton was immense: from 2,000 organisms to the cubic centimetre that existed originally, the density increased to 3,600 after 24 hours, 5,100 after three days, and to 8,000 after a month. The immediate assimilation of the mineral salts by the bacteria of the vegetable plankton allowed an immediate and considerable increase in every sort of fauna. Plaice, for example, grew in thirteen months as much as ordinarily in two or three years. It is true to say that this was merely an experiment and that we may generalize neither its results nor its bearings. All the same, there seems to be something here which is not chimerical, but a technique for the future.'

Since Millport, a pilot experiment has been tried at Lowestoft. The feeding stuff of small fry has been similarly stimulated, and they have been guarded against their natural enemies. The results have been even more remarkable. If we can do as well with potatoes the world's supply of fish and chips is indefinitely assured.

The scientist has other tricks up his sleeve. Where there is water but no cultivable soil, he can grow excellent food in hydroponic tanks. He breeds digestible yeast. He turns seaweed into meringues. He is seeking to cut out the middleman, the wasteful cow, by perfecting a machine that will transmute grass into milk. He is coming very close to the production of synthetic food from minerals.

Theoretically, therefore, there seems no cause to fear that the earth cannot feed all its people. But practice inevitably falls a long way short of theory. The hopeful prospects are nearly all dependent on the application of scientific techniques, on the interlocking abilities of engineers, chemists, nutritional biologists and administrators, and on heavy capital expenditure. We have been thinking in terms of the tycoon with his first hundred thousand behind him. Is it possible in time, to bring these skills and resources to bear in the places where they are most needed? If the size of the planet and the use made of its potential fertility were the only operative factors, the answer could be quick and optimistic. But there is a third, the total population to be fed, and that third makes it an urgent and uncertain race against time.

4

HOW MANY PEOPLE?

INDIA has just begun her third Five Year Plan. Enormous efforts have been made to invigorate the economy of the nation. Special attention has been given to improving farming techniques in the villages. Village co-operatives have bought tractors with government aid and taught young peasants to drive and service them. Specialist teams from the United Nations agencies have made a notable contribution. There have been mistakes and failures, of course, for a slow-moving and deeply traditional economy is not easily galvanized, but the total result is impressive.

It is impressive in terms of annually increasing total national food production. It is bitterly disappointing in terms of available food supplies per head of population. After all the strenuous striving, the position is worse than it was ten years ago. The reason is brutally plain. At the census of 1911 the population of India was 250 millions. At the census of 1951 it was 351 millions. At the census of 1961 it was 438 millions. The mouths are multiplying faster than the food. Commenting on the 1961 returns, Mr Mahommedali Chagla, a former Indian Ambassador to the United States, said in poignant summary: 'What do these figures portend? A dark and dismal future for millions, bitterness and frustration, poverty and unemployment, political discontent and unrest.'

The population explosion, as it is commonly called, is a weapon on the side of poverty and hunger. The demographers tell us somewhat airily that there have been spurts of population before, and that society has always managed to cope with them. But these earlier spurts, as in Victorian

England and America, have as it were been fired by gunpowder. They have followed industrial revolutions. The explosion today is nuclear. It is world-wide, and most spectacularly affecting the economically backward nations.

The simple facts are sobering. The estimated total population of the earth when Jesus was born was 150 millions, slowly climbing to that figure from ten millions in 7000 BC. It doubled in the following six centuries. It doubled again in eight centuries, reaching 600 millions in 1700. The next doubling took only 150 years, and the next only a hundred. The acceleration continues, and so far invariably faster than the forecasters predict. 2,500 millions in 1950 was 3,000 millions in 1960. The 4,000 millions mark will be reached by 1980, and by the end of the century there will be 6,000 million human beings to be fed, clothed and housed.

Perhaps it was because the surge after 1700 happened mainly in developing countries that the experts were so slow to grasp its implications, or perhaps it was because of our natural human disposition to ignore unpleasant possibilities until they become too menacingly near to be ignored any longer. Certainly, only in our generation—after the Rev. T. R. Malthus had apparently been shown up as an ineffectual bogeyman—have we been alerted to the danger. Readers who are now clinging tenaciously, like myself, to the illusion that they are still middle-aged, will remember the slim black volumes of the *Today and Tomorrow* series that stimulated their youth. There were about a hundred of them, each by a writer eminent in his particular field, each with an appropriate title from classical mythology and a sub-title 'The Future of —'. Written between 1924 and 1932, they drew with gusto the shape of things to come, all the way from the future of war to the future of naughty novels. In *Inventing the Future* Professor Dennis Gabor took another look at them, and discovered that not one of them thought of overpopulation. Indeed, J. B. S. Haldane, who led off the series, was worried about declining population.

Nobody speculating today about the year 2000 would be likely to overlook it. He would be much more likely to preach a scientific sermon on the horrors that await the race unless something is done to halt it. The trouble is that it is not due to some phenomenal magnification of human fertility which might be expected to vanish as mysteriously as it arose. Man has altered his own situation. He bred families big enough to survive the quick wastages of death. He is still breeding them, and the pace of wastage has slackened. It is obviously beneficial, and it is comparatively cheap, to reduce infant mortality, to contain epidemics, and to increase the expectancy of life. In the last thirty years the expectancy of life in India has doubled. The child born in 1939 had an average chance of living till he was twenty. The child born today has an average chance of living till he is forty-two. In the same period the death-rate has declined from 30 per thousand to 20 per thousand.

The result is reminiscent of those head-scratching problems set to us in school maths. about how long it would take to fill a tank twenty feet square and ten feet deep if two steady workers were each pouring in a bucket of water every minute and one fast worker was drawing out a bucketful every forty-five seconds. If the third was suddenly slowed down, the amount going in would not vary but the amount going out would fall—and the tank would rapidly fill.

A few years ago I visited British Guiana, and spent a fascinating day with the Italian doctor who rid the colony of malaria. He was a first-class scientist, a brilliant improviser, and a man of profound humanitarian conviction. He observed that the malaria-carrying mosquito common in British Guiana never struck at moving targets. It preferred to attack the sitting or sleeping. So instead of attempting the impossible task of spraying all the water in that vast, hot and excessively damp country, he sprayed buildings.

Within three years the scourge was conquered. He showed me his maps and his tables of comparable statistics with well justified pride.

The victory was dramatically thorough. A disease which enervated and prematurely killed was utterly routed. Those who know anything of the ravages of malaria will have no doubt that it was a splendid and praiseworthy achievement. But the direct consequence is that the population of the colony has doubled within ten years. When I was there, seeing the results of the doctor's devoted labour, development plans were being hopefully and carefully prepared within the narrow limits of the budget of a poor country, eked out by slender external aid. There were plans for agricultural improvement, for the establishment of light industries, for school building and better sanitation. All those plans have been successfully carried through. If the population had been stable there would today be work and hope for all. As it is there is more unemployment, more poverty, more hunger, and the grim pressures are exacerbating the racial tensions that threaten to tear the unhappy nation in two.

What has been said of India and British Guiana could be repeated with infinitesimal variations throughout Asia and the West Indies, and is rapidly becoming true of Africa and Latin America. If the expansion continues to accelerate— and, in the nature of things, it cannot be slowed for a generation, as the children who live longer are already born —will this be a crippling blow to hopes of a richer life for all, or a lethal blow?

Mr Colin Clark, Director of the Agricultural Economics Research Institute at Oxford, is the most noted optimist, and has waged some doughty battles with Lord Boyd Orr. He argues that with the efficient use of known techniques, the earth could feed 28,000 million people, which leaves plenty of margin for developing knowledge after the turn of the century. The hard problem is that of the capital development of the poor countries, but this is not a problem that is inevitably insoluble. He has summarized his argu-

ments in a chapter contributed to an admirable Roman
Catholic symposium, *Christian Responsibility and World
Poverty*, and his conclusion has to be taken very seriously.

We can assume, says Mr Clark, that the rate of population
increase in the economically advanced countries will not
exceed two per cent per annum. These countries have a
rising level of income. They can meet the needs of their
own population growth by setting aside five per cent of the
total national income, but are capable of making average net
savings of ten per cent. The surplus has been used to catch
up the backlog of the depression years and of the second
world war, but the lost ground has by now been largely
covered. It follows that capital will shortly be available on
a really extensive scale for investment in the poorer part of
the world. In brief—though this is a deduction, and not a
statement explicitly made by Mr Clark—we have the means
in spite of population increase to conquer world poverty.
If we fail, it will be a failure of determination and desire.

Sir Charles G. Darwin, the grandson of the world famous
biologist, paints a strikingly different picture. It would not
be far from the mark to comment that he would regard Mr
Clark's calculations as wishful thinking, as projections
which might conceivably happen but which, given the
nature of man as we know him, are most unlikely. One of
the most universal laws of zoology is the law of increase.
When animals are let loose in a new and congenial situation
they multiply until there are so many of them that they
exhaust the food supply. Then the ever-present operations
of natural selection become painfully evident.

Man is an animal who obeys these laws. He is slow-
breeding, and has taken about ten thousand years to get in
sight of the limits, but if he goes on to 10,000 millions by
2050, 20,000 millions by 2100, and 40,000 millions by 2150
he will be jammed hard against them. The FAO conference
in Rome in 1954 sounded the clear note of warning. In
seven years intensive education and the application of
modern techniques raised world food production by eight

per cent, which was an unprecedented achievement. In the same seven years world population rose by eleven per cent. We haven't time to prepare for a future emergency. The emergency is now.

This means, Sir Charles would contend, that we must put away foolish dreams of welfare states and affluent societies. Our own century may live in legend as a fleeting golden age. Life will be a struggle for survival. Only a limited fraction of those born can expect to endure through what we now consider to be a normal life-span. Our kindly, easy charitableness will have to be discarded as too costly a luxury. On the other hand, if we do manage, by a discipline never previously known, to limit human numbers, and so to protect mankind from the searching test of the struggle for life, we may so preserve all inferior genetic mutations that the calibre of man will gradually decline. It sounds very much like: 'Heads, I win, tails, you lose.'

Confronted by expert opinions so contradictory, the normal reaction is to add them together and divide by two. As it happens, the judgement of the overwhelming majority of those who have wrestled with the problem does come about half way. Most would agree with the findings of the committee set up by the British Association for the Advancement of Science to advise the sponsors of the Freedom From Hunger campaign whether or not their project was practicable. If it were made a first priority, said the report, and driven forward by a determined and concentrated effort, it would be possible by the end of the century to lift above subsistence level the estimated population of six thousand millions. Lord Boyd Orr, working on a longer time scale, estimates that it would be possible within eighty years to multiply eightfold food production, and so to feed a likely population of ten thousand millions—with the same proviso about determined and concentrated effort.

None of these moderate judgements, on which we should be wise to rely, will go beyond the cautious phrase 'it is possible'. All strongly suggest that unless the rate of population growth is greatly slowed by the end of their time limits a tragic decline in living standards is almost certain.

Up to a very few years ago it was widely held that there would be a more or less automatic levelling off. The 'theory of demographic transition' was beautifully neat. Primitive societies were balanced by a high birth-rate and a high death-rate. As the struggle for survival began to ease, birth-rates stayed high but death-rates fell. But the social pressures of industrialized and urbanized society develop a new stability with a low birth-rate and a low death-rate. The comforting theory is in fact a generalization from a comparatively brief period of European history. Most of those who are now reading these words will come from small families. Most of them will have grandfathers who come from large families. The Report of the Royal Commission on Population, 1949, gave statistical confirmation to the general impression. From the marriages that took place in England and Wales in 1860, eighty per cent had more than two children and one third (33 per cent) had eight or more. From the marriages that took place in 1925, one third had more than two children and only just over two per cent eight or more.

The pattern of quite startling change was repeated all over Western industrialized society—and some even more startling explanations were devised. Ingenious compilers of statistical correlations demonstrated that fertility declines in direct inverse ratio to the intake of proteins from animal fats. It followed, therefore, that families would shrink as living standards rose. Spots on the sun have been held responsible, as they have for most things. It has been held that the drain on nervous energy which accompanies the artificial life of industrialized communities reduces sexual potency. Soap is a spermicide, so as more soap is used fewer babies are born. Even the bicycle has been blamed. Dennis Wrong, in *Population and Society*, quotes a comment that bicycle riding has a harmful effect on the female reproductive organs.

Prophecy is dangerous in the comparatively new field of demographic analysis, but it is a fairly safe guess that living standards do not affect fertility potential. The change from 1860 to 1925 was social. Children were economic assets at the beginning of the eighteenth century. They started work at six. In a new social situation at the end of the nineteenth century they were economic liabilities. The rent of a more comfortable house, a week's holiday in summer, and a piano in the unused parlour could be afforded more easily with two children or less.

But as the general standards rise the things that had to be skimped and saved for come more easily in reach. There has been a post-war boom in babies in the Western world, and it shows no signs of slackening. All the planning based on the confident prediction that the population had stabilized has proved woefully inaccurate, so that, for example, throughout the West, as we know only too well in Britain, crash programmes are being devised to build new schools, recruit more teachers, and create new universities.

Already tentative explanations of the unexpected development are being given an airing. The soul destroying anonymity of depersonalized mass society has turned men and women back to the warm, personal, enduring satisfaction of home and family. The limitations imposed by genteel, aspiring poverty are removed by affluence. Surrounded by labour-saving gadgets which have taken drudgery out of housework, women are scared by the terrifying boredom of too much leisure, and frustrated because there is insufficient outlet for their energies, so they want bigger families to keep themselves happily and fully occupied.

Whatever the reasons, or complex of reasons, one clear conclusion is that the anticipation of a semi-automatic stabilization of population is far too complacent. The further logical deduction is also clear. If we are able in the next forty or eighty years to lift the needy peoples of the world above the level of subsistence, and to set them on the way to a modest prosperity, we dare not assume that

the higher living standard will of itself slow down permanently the rate of population growth. But unless the rate
is slowed down, one brief generation will see the gleam of
hope before the swift and bitter disappointment of a return
to poverty. The rate must be slowed by deliberate act.

At this crucial point of decision a new and serious problem arises. Plans for the reclamation of land or for increases
in crop production per acre trigger off lively arguments
among the experts, but there is no argument about their
desirability. Christians, Hindus, or agnostics are agreed that
it is a good thing to help the earth to yield more bountifully.
But when we come to the control of population, which is
equally vital, theological differences between Christians introduce a distressing complication. The issue can be simply
—perhaps too simply—stated by quotation from two con-
tributions to the symposium *Our Crowded Planet*. Sir
Julian Huxley wrote: 'Overpopulation is the most serious
threat to human happiness and progress in this very critical
period in the history of the world. . . . Owing to Roman
Catholic pressure, the World Health Organization has not
been allowed even to consider population density as a factor
in world health. Roman Catholicism is barring the adoption
of a birth control policy in many countries, like those of
Latin America, where it is most urgently needed, and is
making it difficult for the United States and other Western
powers to give open or effective support to birth control
measures.' Father Robert Gannon wrote: 'The old Church
has always distinguished between morality and legality, between sin and crime. It has to keep on condemning contraception, not because some Pope or Council forbade it, but
because she still sees it as a violation of the Natural Law,
as a perversion of right order which destroys the meaning-
fulness of the marriage act and creates as many difficulties
as it seeks to avoid, whether moral, physical, psychological,
or merely aesthetic. . . . There are evils worse than malnutrition.'

This is not an academic debate. A campaign against

world hunger must have the willing co-operation of all nations, but it is undeniable that a disproportionally heavy burden of responsibility in the immediate future must rest on the Christian West, simply because the West has the wealth and the technical knowledge. Is the whole-hearted participation of the West to be rendered impossible by a theological controversy?

5

CONTAINING THE
EXPLOSION

THE question that closed the last chapter was misleadingly
simple, but was so framed because it reflects a widespread
popular anxiety. Some sharp critics appear to think that the
Roman Catholic Church is a medieval anachronism, un-
aware of the facts of modern life, which is ignorantly
obstructing human welfare. Others more cynically suggest
that the Church is well aware of the facts but advocates
large families because they supply a large, poor, malleable
membership. There is a little excuse for them, for a few
earnest muddle-headed defenders—the despair of every
Church—insist that she is faithfully proclaiming the divine
command to men to 'be fruitful and multiply', indefinitely
and indiscriminately.

It can be stated quite categorically that these are carica-
tures of informed Roman Catholic teaching. The teaching
—or so it seems to a sympathetic outside observer—has un-
typically wavered between two or three opinions. Sometimes
the emphasis has been on the assertion that the whole earth
is under the good providence of God, and that he will not
permit his creatures to destroy themselves. Sometimes it is
said that we have got our perspective wrong, and that the
real problem is not over-population but under-development.
But the great weight of expert judgement within the Church
frankly agrees that over-population is a looming menace.
The problem is to find the morally right solution.

Here is the real point of controversy between the 'family
planners' and the Roman theologians. The planners see no

other effective possibility than contraception. The Romans are inexorably opposed to contraception. In the remarkable, and in many ways revolutionary, encyclical of July 1961, *Mater et Magistra*, Pope John XXIII made it perfectly clear that artificial contraception was unacceptable.

Behind the flat statement is a logically consistent and carefully articulated argument. It begins with the fundamental proposition that man is not merely a material biological organism. He is intended, by the mercy of God, to live after death in the eternal realm created before the beginning of the world. Parenthood ought, therefore, never to be a casual act, for it initiates for the child that is born a process that extends beyond the bounds of mortal and terrestrial existence. The irresponsible begetting of children outside the bonds of marriage is to be condemned.

The limitation carries no implication that there is something unspiritual and objectionable in the act of sexual intercourse. God has divided his human creation into two sexes, and appointed the way by which the race is continued. Marriage is not an institution that gives a cloak of dubious respectability to an unfortunate necessity, or, as Bernard Shaw once said, 'maximum temptation with the maximum opportunity'. On the contrary, marriage, not entered into lightly or wantonly, is honoured because procreation is so intimate, responsible, and important.

The Roman Catholic Church insists that the primary purpose of marriage is the procreation of children, but does not interpret this in a clinically biological way. The seal of a true marriage is a genuine love between a man and a woman that is reciprocal and sharing and unselfish. The act of intercourse both expresses and strengthens their mutual love, and, at the same time, both opens the way to birth and provides a context of love into which a child may be fittingly born.

As responsibility to the child should prohibit begetting out of wedlock, so it should discourage, within wedlock, the begetting of children who cannot properly be cared for.

Pope Pius XII made the point quite precisely in his address to the Italian Catholic Union of Midwives in 1951. In his lucid expository chapter on 'Family Planning: The Catholic View', contributed to *Christian Responsibility and World Poverty*, Dr John Marshall says so categorically. 'The whole care of the child until it reaches an independent adult life is part of the primary purpose of marriage. This is formally acknowledged in the Canon Law of the Church where it is stated that the primary purpose of marriage is the pro-creation and education of children. If parents are to fulfil this primary purpose properly, the size of their responsi-bilities must be commensurate with their ability to dis-charge them. The regulation of the size of the family to that end is fully in keeping with the Catholic view of marriage.'

Nevertheless, the motive for regulation and the methods employed must be morally sound. If it is probable that the parents would transmit a genetic disability or a physical disease, childlessness is justifiable. If a family is living in such poverty that the birth of many children would keep all hovering on the border line of subsistence, regulation is justified. If regulation can raise a family from poverty to adequate comfort, it is justified. But if the motive is selfish reluctance to accept the responsibilities of parenthood, or a greedy ambition to rise from comfort to luxury, it is not justified. The young couple who cannot afford a baby be-cause they must afford expensive amenities and extravagant recreations are denying the purpose of marriage.

Where regulation is commendable, as it clearly is in many communities, the obvious method is continence. It is not surprising that a Church with a celibate clergy should em-phasize the virtue of restraint, but it would be fair com-ment that among those who have given special study to the question there is a different emphasis. This is not the place for an extended dissertation on sexual psychology, so the point, which is subtly and sympathetically argued by the theologians must be put with crude simplicity. In a happy, established marriage partnership the self-giving of physical union is an important component. Prolonged abstinence can distort the delicate balance of relationship.

The solution, permitting regulation without distorting the marriage relationship, is periodic continence, the use of the 'safe period'. This is based on the theory that the time when a woman can conceive in her monthly cycle is for a comparatively short period after ovulation. The period can be calculated, and avoided by continence. Intercourse between man and wife at other times, the safe periods, is complete, safe, and natural.

The uncompromising opposition to contraception logically follows the assertion that it is incomplete and artificial. By chemical or mechanical means the male sperm is prevented from reaching the female reproductive tract or debarred from the ovum. Contraception and periodic continence are not more or less the same thing. That which is permitted wholly accords with the nature of the sexual act; that which is prohibited changes its nature.

This has been stated as the Roman Catholic attitude because the Roman Catholic moral theologians have analysed the issues most penetratingly and have stated their conclusions most clearly, but it should be added that many Christians of other denominations take the same position. There are those, however, who, going most of the way with the argument, contend that the logic is pressed too hard in the last stage. The safe period method involves meticulously careful calculation, and a deliberate, explicit intention to avoid conception. Is it so very different in principle from contraception?

The expertly technical report on *Human Reproduction*, presented to the British Council of Churches in 1961, implied that it is not. The application of a scientifically devised method is no more 'unnatural' than inoculation. A contraceptive technique is fully permissible, provided that it does not end a life already begun, is freely accepted by both partners, does not endanger the life or health of either partner, and does not limit the psychologically important relational aspect of sexual union.

There is, of course, a reply to this. The Roman moral theologian argues that it confuses ends and means. In any given case, circumstances may justify the intention to avoid procreation. The end is a morally good end. But the end does not justify the means, and if the means employed introduce an artificial and extraneous factor into a Divinely appointed relationship they are not rendered good because the end is commendable.

All this assumes that the means are equally efficacious. It has been forcibly argued that the Roman Catholic Church, bound tight by her own logic, is in fact commending an ineffective means. If indeed there is a fairly precisely predictable safe period, which not all biologists admit, its calculation demands a high degree of educated skill. But where the need for limitation is most urgent, indeed essential for there to be hope of progress, the needed skill is lacking. An experiment to test the validity of the method in Indian villages was, we are told, a complete failure. Dr Marshall, who was quoted earlier, insists that it is fully as reliable as any other method—provided that instruction is given with conscientious care. The difficulty for the Indian women was that they could not follow the instructions. Cardinal Joseph Suenens, probably the outstanding Roman Catholic authority, admits that it cannot be said to be wholly safe. It would be an interesting exercise in casuistry to determine whether, to attain a good end, it is better to use a more commendable and less effective means or a less commendable and more effective.

There is a further complication. Father Lestapis, who was official observer for the Vatican at the World Population Conference in Rome, has analysed carefully the social consequences in those countries where strong official encouragement is given to family planning by contraceptive methods. The most notable is Japan, where he discovers that acceptance of the techniques has been accompanied by a steady rise in the rate of abortions and a steady lowering of moral standards. He traces the same pattern of events in Norway and Denmark. The second, as we may judge from the lively argument now going on in our own country, may be a matter of opinion, but the first is certainly a matter of fact.

The existence of serious and genuine divergence of judgement among Christians on this issue may be regretted, but it must be accepted. It is probable that even if it were to be convincingly demonstrated that the safe period is unsafe—which it has not been—many Christians would feel compelled to conclude, with Father Gannon, that there are worse evils than malnutrition. But at least it is clear that there is no ground for the much too common misconception—if the word may be permitted in this context—that on the principle of population limitation there is irreconcilable opposition all the way. It is, moreover, a sound maxim that where two have the same end in view but cannot journey together all the way, they would be wise to travel in company as far as they can. Bishop James Pike, of the Protestant Episcopal Church of the USA, whose personal judgement comes very close to that of the British Council of Churches report, very sensibly suggested in 1961 that the US National Institute of Health should undertake an extensive research programme to see if the 'rhythm method' could be made as effective as other methods. As he said, all the methods now advocated are hard to teach to backward peoples, and if the safe method pioneered by Dr Ogino and Dr Knaus could be made simpler and more accurate it would probably be the easiest to teach. It would also reduce the unfortunate religious-political opposition which restricts the aid being given to developing countries; an argument without much theological subtlety but with plenty of common sense.

The most recent developments in biochemistry will take the moral theological argument into yet deeper waters. If it proves possible to manufacture a contraceptive pill without harmful side effects, coitus will be perfectly 'natural', fertilization will follow, but nidation will be prevented. (Nidation is the implantation of the fertilized ovum in the lining of the uterus, the process which completes conception.) According to Kenneth Greet and his team of experts this is not abortion, as a woman cannot abort until the fertilized ovum is actually attached to her body. We need not dive further into these particular depths, except to comment that if the point of moral divergence is pushed as far as nidation, logical deduction becomes so refined an technical as to be virtually invisible.

I make no apology for this excursion into a complex and, to some people, disagreeable subject. It is impossible to discuss potential living standards seriously without considering the population problem, and unpardonable evasion to consider that problem without noting the fact of clash of judgement and endeavouring to understand it. Moreover, it has, in passing, introduced a theme to which we must come again. Behind the Roman Catholic position lies the conviction that there is more than one way of interpreting 'living standards', and that not all the interpretations are to be uncritically accepted.

But it still remains true that to ease the burden of poverty where its load is crushing now, and even more to hope to overcome the pressures that might otherwise make it heavier and more widespread in the next half-century, something must be done to contain the population explosion. Even if simple, inexpensive, fool-proof, and morally unexceptionable methods are perfected, it will not be easy. Pride in potency has been deep-rooted through the long centuries in which it was essential to survival. It will be as hard to believe deep down that large families are socially dangerous as it is to recognize that the release of nuclear power has taken the sense out of aggressive nationalism. However, as sense began to dawn when we dangled over the edge of a nuclear inferno, it may also when we are compelled to do simple equations about food available and people to be fed.

It has been done in Japan. As a result of determined,

deliberate, and officially sponsored efforts the birth-rate has declined from 34·3 per thousand in 1947 to 17·5. There were special factors that have to be weighed. Japan is a technically progressive industrialized nation. Her economy was smashed by defeat in the second world war, and she lost almost half her territory. In the five years after the end of the war her population increased by eleven millions, from 72,000,000 in 1945 to 83,000,000 in 1950. There were no empty spaces, and there was no hope of acquiring territory by military aggression.

Japan either had to control the surge, or to collapse under the weight of numbers. The first step was to legalize abortion in 1948, or rather, to be meticulously precise, to declare that it was not illegal under an exceedingly comprehensive list of conditions. But in 1951 the Government instituted an all-out drive for education in methods of birth control. Over eight hundred instruction centres were established and financially supported. The campaign has since been intensified. The authorities claim that the change came when the emphasis switched from abortion to contraception. (The statistics that Father Lestapis used do not go beyond 1956. Since then the abortion rate has declined.)

The death-rate has been halved, the expectation of life increased, and the *per capita* income doubled. The population is still growing. It now stands at 94,000,000 and will probably reach 110,000,000 by 1980. But technological advance can match this slower rate, and no longer pants despairingly in its wake.

It is possible that the next field of sustained effort will be China. The Government of the People's Republic was for years openly contemptuous of the idea that there was any danger in population growth, and seemed rather to be gratified that the most populous nation on earth was adding annually to her manpower. But the bad harvests of 1961 and 1962 have apparently brought about a sudden conversion. It is too soon to examine statistics, even if we could get them, but there has never been any doubt that when the

régime of Mao-Tse-Tung decides to change its mind it does
so with unmistakable thoroughness. And if China presses
on vigorously with education in family limitation, the influence of her example on her semi-satellites in South-East
Asia could be considerable.

India has officially sponsored education in control since
1951, but has never put it high on the list of priorities. Congress, mindful of the complexities of the religious traditions
of India, prefers persuasion to direction; and some of the
older, powerful Congress leaders still believe that the answer
to India's poverty will come from the cornucopia of science
rather than from a fall in the birth-rate.

The United Nations Economic and Social Council has
recently been organizing surveys in preparation for a World
Population Conference in 1965, and, with the terrifying
comprehensiveness of a UN agency that has a top-level
occasion in its sights, has been proliferating sub-committees.
The Afro-Asian nations, who come fairly new to them, may
in consequence come to the conclusion that population control is the progressive and therefore proper thing to do.
Sometimes a little emulative vanity can get results where
sober reason fails.

But, on the whole, it looks as though the race is going to
be a very close thing. The experts know the danger. The
people, who produce the babies, do not. It is not so certain
that the race will be lost that the effort must be abandoned
in despair, or doggedly pursued with the dispiriting inner
conviction that it is the right course but foredoomed to
defeat. It is not so certain that the race will be won that
effort can be relaxed.

6

SATANIC MILLS

I SPEND my holidays in a tiny village in South Devon, a cluster of white-walled thatched cottages just off the tourist track. When I preach in the little Methodist chapel, the hand-written poster disdains such descriptions as 'President of the Methodist Conference' or 'General Secretary of the Christian Citizenship Department'. Firmly putting first things first, it says 'now residing at Hillside Cottage'.

It would be hard to find a place in these islands more remote from the frenzies of Westminster. But the life of the village no longer depends wholly on the big farms. Once upon a time, and not so long ago, the biggest farm of all employed thirty men for three weeks to get the harvest in, given good weather. The farm is bigger now, but four men bring in the harvest in three days, with machines. The young men of the village go by bus or motor-cycle to work in Plymouth.

Britain cannot from her own land feed all her people, as we are sharply reminded in time of war, but agricultural productivity is steadily rising as the agricultural labour force is steadily falling. Through all the divagations and diversions of this study so far, we have been concentrating on the basic questions of feeding the expanding population of the world. The emphasis has been on actual and potential crops. But, in fact, the real question is not how we are to feed the hundreds of millions of peasant farmers who live on the land. It is rather how we are to get them off it. There are too many people already on it to give modern farming techniques a chance of success, and not enough off it to provide the ancillary services that are also essential to a modestly comfortable living standard.

If other employment could be found for at least half the fellahin of Egypt, both they and those who remained on the farm would be better off. At present an individual family subsists on a couple of acres. The incessant pressures of poverty mean, as we have previously noted of India, that the ground is over-worked and under-fed. They also mean that it is inefficiently worked by the cheap muscle-power of the family.

Family holdings are smaller still in Turkey; only just over one acre. The FAO Report on Turkey said flatly that very many of the nine million agricultural labourers were super-fluous, and continued: 'These excess workers increase the danger of soil being tilled that should not be tilled and of overgrazing by livestock which they are trying to raise; they bring about further fragmentation of the land and aggravate the reprehensible practice of clearing forests for pasture by the expedient of burning down the trees. Draining off this useless manpower from the villages must therefore take the highest priority in any programme aimed at overcoming the structural crisis in Turkey.'

The remedy is not popular. It is criticized as a perverse disdain of the primary and necessary service of agriculture, and the lot of the poorest peasant is compared favourably with that of the rootless proletarian compelled to sell his labour for a pittance in a factory. Life that moves with the slow, satisfying rhythm of the seasons is contrasted with life dominated by the inhuman pounding of machinery. When he is well warmed up to his theme, the critic can see in the hideous advance of the dark, satanic mills the defeat of the spirit of man. The countryman in the heart of most of us sympathizes—until we compel ourselves to recognize the realities of the actual life of the under-nourished peasant. The mills need not be dark or satanic, and the reward of the labourer need not be a pittance. Nor is the advocacy of industrialization the product of contempt for agriculture.

The plain fact is that the presence of too many people on the land reduces the supply of food. Apart altogether from the necessity to develop other forms of production, agriculture itself will remain a depressed and inefficient activity so long as between seventy and eighty per cent of the working population of the under-developed nations is employed in it. The concept of a world predominantly rural has its attractions, but to get a rural world that fed all its people adequately we should have to halve the present population and hold the total down to that level. The only practical alternative to selective extermination is to find other jobs.

But is the practical alternative a possible alternative? How are these other jobs to be found? The technical problems are immense, but are not insoluble. The natural tendency to dramatically impressive simplification, to see the issue symbolized in the contrast between a bouncing Western baby and a pot-bellied, starving African child, stirs compassion but falsifies reality. The pockets of near destitution are tragic, but are comparatively small. It is necessary to remind ourselves continually that the dominant problem is malnutrition, not starvation; energy-sapping illness, not painful death; illiteracy, not ignorance; need, not destitution. From the point of view of economic strength the nations are not grouped into the two camps of the rich and the poor. They are more like the struggling line of runners in a cross-country race, with those in front going well and those behind either catching up or falling back.

W. W. Rostow, in *The Stages of Economic Growth*, describes those who are plodding painfully in the rear and steadily losing ground as the countries still in the stage of 'traditional society'. Those which have managed to get clear of the tail are in the 'pre-condition stage'. If they keep going and are able to pull out a little more speed, they enter the 'take-off stage' and come in sight of the leaders.

Paul G. Hoffman, who supervised the successful Marshall Plan and is now deeply committed to the United Nations Development Decade, hammers away at the idea that economic progress must be pictured in these dynamic terms. If a quarter of the human race on firm ground had to haul three-quarters out of the sinking sands of destitution, they would strive in vain. But if the furthest laggard in the cross-country race is moving, however slowly, something can be done.

Hoffman gives three illustrative examples in *World Without Want*. The Republic of Togo is a new and primitive nation, with few roads, few schools, poor crops and virtually no industry. The average income per head of its population is well under a hundred dollars a year. Aid from UN and France is going to the basic essentials: agriculture, education and roads. Togo is a long way behind, but is moving. Colombia has graduated to the pre-condition stage. The country is still predominantly agricultural, but diversification of industry has started. Special training programmes on such things as warehouse management, government administration, and inland fisheries are producing a trickle of experts. Average income is up to about 250 dollars a year. In short, there is a tiny margin for saving and capital expansion. India is very nearly through the pre-condition stage. Industry is making good progress. The great potential resources of the sub-continent, and the will to modernization of her leaders, have to contend with the immensity of her present poverty. (*Per capita* income is as low as 65 dollars a year.) But by planned effort India is setting aside 3,000 million dollars a year for development. She needs 1,000 million dollars a year of outside investment and aid, but anticipates that within a decade her own export earnings and savings will square the bill. That will be the day of 'take off'. The late Pandit Nehru believed that in 1973 the 'eternal compulsory fast' would begin to come to an end.

Paul Hoffman is plugging a campaign, and is inclined to optimism. He writes much more in the spirit of what might be and what ought to be than of what is likely to be. If only aid were generous, speedy, and co-operatively given by the nations working together, twenty struggling nations could have self-sustaining economies by 1970, and, as each ceased to be helped and became a helper, the whole family of nations could be freed from poverty by 2000. It would mean that for at least the next ten years seventy per cent of the capital required for economic development would have to come from the wealthy nations, but all of it would not amount to five per cent of what is being spent on military defence.

The trouble is that if we had the sort of world which would respond with unselfish generosity to such an appeal it would not be the sort of world which would need an appeal. The percentages are calculated accurately enough; as accurate as the appeals which tell us so frequently that a particular worthy cause could be adequately financed by gifts equivalent to a packet of cigarettes. The wealthy nations prefer to spend their money on themselves.

The hard fact is that in the ten years between 1950 and 1960 the poorer countries actually lost ground. The rate of growth for their exports was 3.6 per cent, the rate of growth for their imports 4.6. Most of the exports of the developing countries, their money-earners, are primary commodities, like rubber and cotton and cocoa. Prices in 1960 were just about the same as in 1950. Their imports, the money-spenders, are mainly finished goods. Prices for them were markedly higher. So in terms of trade, in receipt for exports set against payment for imports, they were at the end of the ten years about nine per cent worse off. Their share in total world trade in 1950 was thirty per cent. In 1960 it was twenty per cent.

Even though the decade was one of expanding population and increasing world consumption of goods, the trend should cause no surprise. The main reason, in my own judgement, is the operation of the law of 'to him that hath', though, possibly out of deference to the susceptibilities of the nations so adversely affected, the UN experts put it well down in their list. The advanced countries are fighting for markets from positions of strength. They can sell fibres,

C

minerals, and even many classes of foodstuffs more cheaply. In direct competition with a 'pre-condition' nation they win much more often than they lose.

They also take elaborate care to blunt the edge of competition in their own home markets. The developing country that tries to stabilize its economy by developing manufacture has to surmount the barricades of tariffs, quotas and internal taxes before it can get a foothold inside. After a decade of golden eloquence about the imperative necessity for a free flow of trade, the barricades still stand. In 1960 the developing countries had no more than 5·6 per cent of global trade in manufactured goods. They did manage, it is true, to lift their total exports of such goods by four per cent. The industrialized countries boosted theirs by eight per cent.

It was, I think, the late Will Rogers (no relation), who said that the human mind never moves faster than when it sees the prospect of a quick profit. But despite the elaborate devices of human ingenuity in this pursuit, which add so many complications and conditional clauses to applied economics, it is still basically true that in the long run prices depend on the interaction of supply and demand. The poor nations have the rough end of the price deal because there is a declining demand for their primary products. A production manager in England or West Germany rejoices in a technological development that cuts costs by economizing on materials. The supplier of the materials is not so happy when tin-plate uses less tin and generators use less fuel.

The supplier is in a worse plight when an alternative material can be created. Synthetic fibres have taken a great bite out of the market once exclusively reserved for silk, cotton, wool and linen. Leather is being pushed out by plastics. More synthetic rubber than natural rubber was produced in 1962.

This is a predictable outcome in a competitive and changing world market. Any remedial measures must move in the direction of controlling competition. It is not beyond the bounds of possibility. Political argument and military confrontation between the chunk of the planet that calls itself 'free' and the chunk that calls itself 'communist' have, among other things, established the simple delusion that one side firmly believes in free competition and the other equally firmly in State regulation. There is, of course, a profound distinction between the two types of economics. One is primarily geared to the demands of the consumer, the other to the plans of the producer. But on each side there is in fact a good deal of common ground and parallel method. Both have been compelled to find a middle way between the paralysing rigidity of over-meticulous control and the anarchy of unrestricted competition. Proposals to limit the violence of competition in world trade to help the developing nations may be obstructed or watered down by selfishness, but they will not automatically be ruled out of court as doctrinally obscene.

The obvious first step is to tackle the fluctuations in the prices of primary commodities. At the New Delhi Assembly of the World Council of Churches I was appointed to a sub-committee that was instructed to suggest practical ways in which the social witness of the Church could be manifested. It was a large assignment, but we were not dismayed. We began, without admitting it, by quoting selections from our more effective sermons. We were brought down to earth by a Malayan layman. How could his church plan social service when his people never knew from one year to the next what their income would be? They relied on the rubber plantations, and rubber prices were fixed thousands of miles away in New York. He was right. Between 1950 and 1962 the price of natural rubber rose as high as 1,024 dollars a ton and fell as low as 432 dollars a ton. We failed to solve his problem, but some of us began to think much more seriously about it.

Already for some commodities, such as wheat, sugar, and tin, export prices have been stabilized by international agreement. The range could be extended. Compensation schemes, using the techniques of insurance, could cushion exporters against the catastrophic losses incurred when the bottom falls out of the market. The advanced nations could abolish or reduce tariffs and discriminating quotas, without demanding some equivalent concession; or at least they could weight the odds for a specific period of years on a sliding scale.

The developing nations could show more enterprise. They have tended to assume that the world owes them a living, and that the living ought to be handed to them on a plate. They are still relying on products no longer needed in former quantities because of technological development or the invention of new synthetics, and relying on the former markets. They should diversify their products, seek new uses for the old ones, develop trade with each other, and push harder the stuff they have to sell.

The first step would help by reducing the rate at which the under-developed countries are losing ground, but would do little more. There is not enough demand for their raw materials to pay for the development they need. Somehow or other the export of manufactured and semi-manufactured goods must be encouraged. Everybody warmly agrees that an expansion of world trade caused by rising living standards would benefit them all, but the vision of prosperity in a richer world fades sharply at the quixotic suggestion that Britain or America should deliberately handicap their own salesmen to help the poor. Textile manufacturers and unions deeply sympathize with the refugees of Hong Kong, but have very strong views on the importation of cheap cotton goods from the Hong Kong mills. But there is no getting away from it. If the nations where poverty is endemic are to escape from poverty they must improve their agriculture and reduce the agricultural working population. They must create the ancillary structures essential to an industrialized or semi-industrialized society, and pay for them out of the profits of industry. That means direct competition with the industrial nations, in which they have next to no hope of success unless their competitors make it easy for them.

In preparation for a United Nations Conference on Trade and Development, specifically intended to seek practical aid for the less developed countries, the Preparatory Committee laid particular stress on the obligations to be accepted by those that needed help. Governments—such as those of the East African or Central American nations—should explore the possibilities of 'common markets'. They should provide incentives to exporters; long term credit at low rates, subsidies, and tax relief. The potentially generous importers were assured that the bread they cast on the waters would rapidly return to them transformed into cake, or, in the staider language of UN, 'additional earnings obtained from such exports would be spent largely on increased imports from the industrialized countries, and thus in the long run the latter countries would benefit'. But there was no disguising the fact that this would not be trading on a reciprocal basis. The late developers—if another euphemism may be permitted, to make a change—would have to be given special privileges.

To those who flatly refuse to get excited about economics, all this may sound extremely dreary but basically reasonable. Unfortunately, it merely lifts the 'vicious circle' to a higher level. To take the opportunity offered, the poorer nations would have to industrialize and to expand the complex apparatus of commerce. If it was operating on a scale big enough to be really effective they would be able to pay for it out of income—but they need the income now in order to get started. Talking about export market guarantees is rather like giving good advice on the investment of share dividend to a man who cannot afford to buy the shares. Initially, and for some years to come, the equipment for development programmes—for machinery, buildings, and training—will have to be paid for by external financial aid.

Chancing a speculative investment that might pay handsomely later on, private foreign investors might be ready to help, if they had some confidence that their investment would be protected. Expropriation of the assets of the 'neo-colonialist exploiters' gives a heady satisfaction to an inexperienced and newly independent administration, but it can be costly in the long run.

Until there is a measure of stability and some evidence of local enterprise, foreign firms that take big risks will want big profits; and struggling nations are understandably reluctant to let big profits travel abroad. So most of the essential initial capital aid will have to come from foreign governments. Again it can be said that there are no insuperable technical problems. Apart from the national enterprises developed as cold war instruments for influencing the uncommitted countries, United Nations is responsible for at least fifteen special agencies, such as the International Bank for Reconstruction and Development and the International Monetary Fund, which have worked out all the mysterious financial techniques involved. But the ingenious plans of the international accountants for capital grants and capital loans and long-term amortizations all depend on one thing: the willingness of the wealthy nations to finance competitors, to set them up in business and then to give them special trading advantages.

It would be a considerable understatement to say that the demand for generosity of this sort and in this field has not quite the appeal of a plea for a gift for a starving child. The Freedom From Hunger campaign has evoked a fine response. The United Nations Development Decade is more than halfway through, and after six years not one person in a thousand has even heard of it. Being in a position to help the under-privileged can give a warm glow to the helper, but subsidizing a competitor is asking a lot of hard-headed business men. Is it asking too much?

7

SHORT SUPPLIES?

I T is a fair comment, and not simple cynicism, that to ask
hard-headed business men to subsidize potential competitors
may be to put too severe a strain on their natural benevolence. Their response will depend on the quality of the
intelligence inside the hard heads. But before we move on
to that particular problem there is another vital question
to be asked and answered. Is it asking too much of the
planet?

To summarize briefly, we have so far been looking at the
possibility of helping the inhabitants of the world's poorest
countries to rise to a modestly adequate living standard. The
first stage target is the sort of standard that could be roughly
assessed in terms of an annual average income per head of
about 200 dollars. It would be possible if before the end of
the century the curve of the rise in population could be
flattened, if more land could be put under better cultivation,
and if surplus population could be drained from the land
into diversified industry.

This is not a theoretical analysis. It is, in fact, a condensed
and simplified account of the history of the economically
advanced nations. Beneath the obvious and often-discussed
surface differences, it was the way taken by England after
the Napoleonic Wars, America after the Civil War, and
Russia after the October Revolution. In all three the transition involved painful social disruption and much individual
suffering; in the first two by misguided respect for the 'iron
laws' of Ricardian economics, in the third by misguided
respect for the 'iron laws' of Marxist economics—for the
basic pattern was the same. It is the way now being taken by

India and Brazil. If we have the wisdom to learn from the hard lessons of the past it may be a smoother way for Africa and Asia, but it will still essentially be the same way.

It means tinned foods, bicycles, radio sets, electric cookers, and power driven factories. The potential skill is present. We have already discovered the remarkable aptitude of the African as a mechanic in the least developed areas of the continent, and should have no doubt about the capabilities of the Chinese. Capital and training could do the trick. But will there be enough raw material and sources of power to meet the demands of an industrial world?

In an earlier chapter I wrote of the fertile land reduced to desert by human folly and rapacity, but it is land that can carefully and patiently be nursed back to health. Once the mineral resources of the planet have been plundered they cannot be put back again. The figures are startling. On the most cheerful estimates, if world consumption continues at its present rate, supplies of zinc, tin, lead and copper will probably be exhausted by the end of the century. Taking into account the additional demand from increasing population and more widespread industrialization, the supplies will almost certainly be exhausted by that time. The 'probably' and the 'almost' are cautious reservations, allowing for the possible but unlikely discovery of extensive new deposits.

Iron is, fortunately, more plentiful. Taking into account the virtual certainty that technical advance will permit the economic use of low-grade ore, there is enough to keep us going for a thousand years. The bauxite ore which is the source of aluminium should hold out for at least a couple of centuries. There are more abundant supplies of the light, strong, adaptable metal, titanium, than was once imagined; but if it is pressed into service as a substitute it would not fill the tin and copper gap for more than three or four hundred years.

Industrial man will have to learn to be more economical in his use of metal, and more resolute in recovering and converting scrap. But the prospect is not so grim as it appears. Just as what once were thought to be the inexhaustible treasures of the earth are running out, the chemist is synthetizing. It is not, after all, essential that car bodies and saucepans should be made of metal. This is a race that the scientist is winning. The new factories of the world after the Second Industrial Revolution will not be the grimy, slag-heap surrounded fortresses of the First; but that is no cause for tears.

The new hives of industry, light and airy, functionally designed, built of glass fibre and plastic, will not look in the least like the mastodons of the Black Country, but they will be serving the same purpose. They will be factories. The progress of industrialization will not be abruptly halted by a shortage of raw materials.

But will it be stopped for lack of available power to drive the machines? My own impression, before I began to dive into the intricate statistical calculations of the fuel experts, was that supplies of coal and natural oil were rapidly dwindling, but that there was no need for anxiety because the harnessing of the atom would provide all the power required for millennia to come. After the dive, which I do not propose to describe in detail, the impression was considerably modified.

There may have been a touch of self-delusion in the forecasts of the gloomier sages of the early 1950s; an anxiety to explore speedily the possibilities opened up by the nuclear physicists. The power planners of the Common Market countries dramatically insisted that atomic energy would be needed not much later than 1975 to make good the coming coal and oil shortages. In fact, and even if expanding industry increases the demand tenfold, known coal reserves will last for a thousand years. The likelier probability is that the use of coal will diminish. One very recent estimate is that in the United States, the Soviet Union, and China there is enough to last for 250,000 years.

The future of oil is less predictable. On one hand, the

rise in the rate of consumption is consistently steeper than the estimates. On the other hand, every time the day when the wells will run dry has been confidently computed colossal new reservoirs have been found. The oil industry is only as old as the century. The spectacular growth of the industry has understandably given rise to fears that it will decline as quickly as it has grown, but the fears are not justified. The present levels of consumption could be stepped up sixtyfold and will should still have some in reserve in 2000.

Atomic power will be more slowly developed than the first enthusiasts thought. Breeder reactors using nuclear fission have been developed, and are effective though expensive still compared to oil and coal. But disposing of the inevitable radio-active waste presents a serious problem. Pit-banks and slag-heaps are bad enough. Mounting stocks of unwanted, unusable, undisposable, radio-active sludge are too horrible to contemplate.

Extensive examination of the technical problems in the commercial application of nuclear physics is not essential to this study—which makes a pleasant change. Those best qualified to judge are agreed that the ultimate solution lies in the control of nuclear fusion; the H bomb instead of the A bomb. Once the very formidable technical difficulties are overcome, we shall have a 'clean' product and at last a virtually inexhaustible source of power. But all the indications are that we shall be into the twenty-first century before that stage is reached.

A good deal could be done to increase the supply of hydro-electric power, with the added advantage that taming the wild rivers facilitates the irrigation and cultivation of the hitherto unused land on the river banks. In the lands where the sun shines, which are for the most part the lands of greatest poverty, significant developments are taking place in the storage of solar energy.

In short, to this last doubting question based on the limited resources of Earth, it is possible without much tincture of speculative optimism to return an encouraging reply. Our world can provide the raw materials and the energy to afford to an increasing population a rising standard of living. Whether the standard is attained or not depends on the will of man, not on the niggardliness of Nature.

8

ALTERNATIVE TO WAR

B y deliberate design my approach up to this point has been a slow progress from problem to problem. I have tried to tackle them as they came, honestly and objectively and without presuppositions; not arguing a case, but allowing each set of facts to lead on to the next. The real subject under discussion is not aid to developing countries, or the potentially cultivable acreage of the planet, or any other such blanket generality, but the prospect of a decent standard of life for our fellow men and women. It is not a subject for the exercise of benevolent wishful thinking. We need to soak in the facts before we dare make any promises.

As might have been expected, precise answers could not be given to all the questions, and some very wide margins had to be allowed for error in assessing the facts, but there is not much doubt about the conclusion. Breaking the back of poverty and hunger will be no soft option, but the enterprise is not foredoomed to failure. To avoid the escape route of unnecessary imprecision, I kept my mind firmly fixed to the year 2000. The world population will have soared to six thousand millions. They can be adequately fed, housed, clothed and educated, and lifted to that level above bare subsistence which is the beginning of reasonable hope, from the natural resources of the earth and the technical skills of man. They can be—but that is not to assert that they will be.

The agricultural and industrial revolutions that will be necessary will demand a revolution in the minds of those now shackled by poverty. The conservatism of peasantry, bred by generations of traditional adaptation to the environment of poverty, is a phenomenon that has perpetually checked and infuriated reformers. Nearly half a century after the Bolshevik Revolution. Mr. Krushchev is still engaged in threatening and cajoling the obstinately traditional farmers of the Soviet Union.

One can sympathize with the peasants. The change to a new way of life is an act of faith, and most of us prefer the devil we know to the devil we don't know. The change to an industrial-modern agricultural way is a transition from poverty and stability to possible prosperity and possible collapse. The stakes are higher, but so are the risks. The wars that have smouldered, burst into sudden flame, and then smouldered again in South-East Asia would have smashed the fabric of an advanced society, but they do not smash the tougher, time-woven, peasant fabric of Laos or Viet-nam. The scepticism of the man who farms as his great-grandfather did is strengthened every time a hasty reformer comes a cropper. Somebody had the bright idea that windbreaks would protect the grain in the vast flat lands of Russia. They also protected the insects which thereupon ravaged the crops—and confirmed the peasants' unflattering opinion of the experts. The elaborately and expensively organized ground-nuts scheme charged at the tsetse-fly infested scrub of Tanganyika like a military assault. The flies died, but so did the bees. The bare land lost its water. If this is modern farming, the suspicious African reflected, I'll stick to what I know.

The bonds of tradition and the inertia of malnutrition are formidable obstacles, but they must not be exaggerated. The sacrifices that African and Asian peasants make to give the opportunity of even rudimentary education to their children, and the voracity with which those children snatch at the crumbs from the table of learning, flatly and convincingly contradict those who say that the poor are perfectly content to stay as they are. Africans in Kenya are turning out to be excellent, careful, and thoroughly up-to-date coffee farmers. The streets of London and Birmingham and Bradford are crowded with people who saw a chance of escaping from poverty and plunged into an alien environment to seize that chance. Despite the severities of apartheid and the indignities of third-class citizenship, thousands cross illegally into the Union of South Africa to improve their material conditions. In fact, the psychological revolution has already taken place. Much of the world's turbulence, the 'green revolution' that the Red politicians are trying to divert to their own political ends, is the revolt of unsatisfied desires. The fatalistic apathy which is adaptation to inevitable poverty is fading the world over.

The selfishness and wilful ignorance of the affluent presents a much tougher problem than the inertia of the poor. The wealthy artisan—wealthy in comparison with the majority of mankind—in London or Moscow or Melbourne may be kept awake at night by indigestion or unrequited love, but he rarely loses any sleep because destitute beggars die every night in the streets of Calcutta. For many in the West poverty is not very far behind them. As a boy in Lancashire I tasted at second-hand the bitterness of poverty in the stories told to me by my elders. There is, understandably, more of a mixture of satisfaction with the present and apprehension that the bad old days might return than concern for the lot of others far away.

There is, moreover, a fear that improving the conditions of the desperately needy might weaken the security of the comparatively comfortable. The landlord and the moneylender do not want to lose their power over the chronically hard-up peasant. The stoutest resistance to raising rates of pay for African miners in the Northern Rhodesian Copperbelt and to opening to them a higher grade of employment came from the well-paid members of the white trade unions.

No doubt the unions, as corporate organizations, could take up attitudes more deplorably selfish than the individual members have publicly permitted themselves. Certainly the corporate aggregation which is a nation is unashamedly self-regarding. The aid that is given to the under-developed has strings attached. It has been used as a weapon in cold war strategy. It flows more easily to generals than to headmasters. The politicians in the United States Congress are less inhibited and less hypocritical than their counterparts in other assemblies when they angrily protest about feeding the mouth that bites them, but their counterparts act more discreetly on the same principles. If proof is needed that performance lags far behind promise, one has only to compare the eloquent tributes to the inception of the United Nations Development Decade with the tardy and pathetic response in hard cash.

The problem, therefore, is to find an incentive sufficiently powerful, either in attraction or menace, to galvanize the wealthy nations into vigorous action and to quicken the poor into less suspicious co-operation. I firmly believe that there is such an incentive; one that appeals alike to fear, to prudence, and to noble resolve. It is to envisage the campaign against world poverty and hunger as an alternative to war between the nations. This sounds, I know, most naïvely unworldly and idealistic. In fact, the unworldly ones are the pre-nuclear romantics, priding themselves on their realism and still parroting the clichés of a world order that is passing.

In the first place, the alternative is genuine. As I battled with estimates and calculations before writing the preceding chapters, it became depressingly clear to me that to tackle world poverty with any hope of modest success was no casual, part-time enterprise. There are so many people to be fed, so much land to be reclaimed and restored, so much training to be given in agricultural techniques, such vast sums of financial aid required, such complexity in the allocation of the aid, such a host of essential technicians—and all to be done so quickly if it is not to be done in vain. If they were efficiently mobilized there are enough resources, skill and manpower in the world to accomplish the colossal task; but not enough both to do it and to fight each other.

Britain and France have been among the most generous

givers of aid, but the first enormous charge on French resources is the bill for her *force de frappe*. The help that Britain gives comes from the residue after £2,000 million has been spent on defence. The United States is the most generous of all, but she is cutting down her aid because the burden of defence costs is intolerably heavy. The choice is straightforward and inescapable, involving at bottom only the most elementary axiom of economics, the art or science of allocating scarce resources. To build and maintain the counter-stroke force implicit in nuclear warfare demands an economic effort of unparalleled magnitude. To mobilize a living standards campaign on a realistic scale means either adding or substituting another economic effort that would parallel the magnitude. The sober truth is that the world cannot afford both.

It does not automatically follow, of course, that if the governments of East and West had the sense to negotiate a general and comprehensive disarmament they would switch their expenditure to tractors and harvesters and grants without strings. They might well prefer to soar from comfort to luxury at home, doling out from time to time a little easily spared and ineffective charity. But they would be incredibly stupid and short-sighted if they thought that that particular shot was on the table. Disarmed nations wallowing in plenty in a world of misery would be asking for trouble, and would get it. They will get it even if they stick to their arms.

Let me repeat once more that I am thinking about possibilities during the next forty years, not balancing propositions in a timeless and bloodless abstraction. Ours is a messy, untidy, patchwork world. Half a dozen contradictory contradictions can be immediately adduced to every confident generalization about it. But for the last forty years or so, every major political problem, and most others, could be connected with what was normally and inaccurately called the East-West conflict. It has been a curious and desperately dangerous amalgam of old-fashioned power politics and half-baked ideologies. Every strike in Western industry and every movement for colonial freedom was attributed to Communist agitators. Every breakdown of Soviet planning or satellite discontent with Russian imperialism was attributed to capitalist reactionaries. American missiles are beamed on Russia, Russian on America. Senators have denounced 'socialized medicine'; the Central Committee of the Communist Party have fulminated against jazz. It was a ramifying but overt contest, each of the two titanic adversaries seeking to persuade or coerce the allegiance of the uncommitted. The contest is very probably coming to an end. The kaleidoscope of international relationships is settling to a new pattern.

The main reason, in my opinion, is that the Soviet Union has joined the select circle of the affluent nations. The revolutionary fervour has waned. She has too much to lose to risk swapping ICBMs across the Atlantic or the Arctic Circle. She is certainly ready to quarrel with China in order to begin to come to an understanding with the United States. It is a reluctant understanding, enforced by the distasteful realities of nuclear warfare. But when an American President is assassinated by a Marxist newly returned from Russia, and instead of a strident call to war there is cool, intelligent appraisal of the situation by the American press and public, it is clear that things have greatly changed.

It is to be hoped that the understanding, which is in the interest of both great powers, will grow, for it pushes away from the world for the first time since 1945 the immediate threat of nuclear devastation. But as yesterday's problem is slowly and painfully resolved, tomorrow's begins to loom. China, declaring that the Soviet Union has capitulated to the capitalists, claims the revolutionary leadership of the toiling and exploited masses.

Dimly foreshadowed is a world tragically divided in a new way; not between conflicting, blurred ideologies but starkly between the rich and the poor, the white and the coloured. It may not happen. Africans are not impressed when the pale Chinese offer themselves as 'coloured brethren'. They are too proud of their new independence to surrender it easily, and not yet sophisticated enough to fall for the propaganda lines that trap the intellectuals. Chinese aggression in the high Himalayas has alienated India. Chinese influence in Indonesia led directly to the creation of the counter-state of Malaysia. Nevertheless, the possibility of the new division is so real that simple prudence should encourage the 'haves' to raise the standards of the 'have-nots'; the whites to recognize and foster the human dignity of the coloured.

This is argument put deliberately on the lowest level of self-preservation and self-regard. If the gap between rich and poor continues to widen, and if the world does polarize into two opposing camps, the almost certain outcome will be war. From that point the estimation of probabilities moves into the realm of science-fiction—where it had better stay. The advanced nations could win a nuclear war, ending, if they were lucky, with a world crippled, decimated in population, and pock-marked with lethal radio-activity. The poorer nations could by force of numbers win a conventional war, dragging down the West to the level of their own poverty, and in the terrible enterprise destroying for generations their own prospect of escape from its thrall. Either prospect is grim. A serious, urgent campaign against poverty is the alternative to war.

The low-level argument may at least persuade the hard-headed gentlemen that long-term credits to developing countries at low interest could offer better security than cohorts of expensive nuclear missiles beamed in the wrong direction, and as these are the gentlemen who will have to be persuaded before the campaign can really get going it would be as well to press the argument hard. But on other and higher levels intelligence and compassion move in the same direction.

Save for a few psychopaths, all people everywhere are agreed that war is evil. It is detested and feared—but it exerts a strange attraction. Beneath the undeniable danger, hardship and suffering in the last war there was an oddly stimulating sense of participation in a great enterprise. Far below the genuine and heartfelt rejoicing at the return of peace there was an oddly disconcerting sense of deflation. We hate war, but it is exciting and demanding. We love peace, but it is by comparison flat and insipid.

It seems very likely that after six thousand years or so of refining ways of bashing the life out of adversaries man has at length devised a scientific method of massacre that will rob war of its compensatory companionable excitement. He needs an alternative. The trouble has been that he has not yet found one. Peace as it is commonly understood is not at all the alternative to war. It is the absence of war, the time when the bombers are grounded and the destroyers moth-balled, the breathing-space between the rounds. The quite appalling truth is that war dominates the human imagination as positive and vigorous activity. Peace is too pallid and negative to stir the heart or set the pulses throbbing.

All of which, of course, is thoroughly bad theology. Peace is, or ought to be, as vigorous and positive as war and in-finitely more attractive. One is the purposive organization of men, materials, and skills to destroy. The other is the purposive organization of men, materials, and skills to create. Both stretch to the limit human intelligence, endur-ance and courage. Both weld in a common aim a vast variety of abilities and services. In theory, that is to say, peace is the opposite to war. In practice, it has never had so stirring and stimulating a content, so precise an objective.

Man is an aggressive and practical creature. He will respond to a challenge, provided that it is definite enough for him to get to grips with. Ask him to organize a sales promotion drive, or to build a church in a new area, or to navigate a submarine through an enemy minefield, and he will grumble happily as he gets on with the job. Other things being equal, he would prefer to do a job with an end product worth achieving; but if other things are not equal, if one demand is plain and another verbosely uncertain, it is the plain demand that has the pull.

It seems to me that the winding road of human history has reached a fork of quite unprecedented significance. Every generation, of course, is convinced that no other has had to face its own difficulties and opportunities; and every generation has been right so to think. But it is surely true that the choices before our own generation are more than intensifications of the choices of the past. For the first time in all the life of men on earth he has the power to destroy the planet on which he lives. For the first time the sheer growth in the numbers of his kind puts his future in danger. For the first time he is factually aware of the extent of poverty. For the first time he has the technical capacity to end poverty. This is not rhetoric. It is realism. It sounds unreal simply because the situation is so new.

It is the conjunction of all these revolutionary novelties that makes a definite and constructive peace-making, in our generation, the sort of choice that can be in every respect what William James called a 'moral alternative to war'. For centuries visionaries have been dreaming up ingenious devices to divert man's natural pugnacity away from self-destruction. Charles Fourier thought it could be done by arranging global competitions to discover the best maker of omelettes. Others—who can never have watched Rangers play Celtic—hoped that sport could do the trick. As they must have known in their hearts, alternatives of this calibre are bound to be pathetically ineffectual. Inventive, aggressive, organizing man can do them in his spare time with his spare energy. But with providential timing the concept of an onslaught on world poverty just fits the bill. It is on the same scale as war. It puts up technical problems and logistic problems tough enough to keep ingenuity at full stretch. The complications are absorbing. The purpose is clear and desirable, and the pressures for action urgent.

Possibly my picture of man as a creature restlessly seeking for a practical cause that will test his wits and challenge his courage is exaggerated, but not, I think, unduly so. It may be that it is the men and women a little above the average, the prodders and pushers and drivers and leaders, whom I have most in mind. But the fact that the mass of mankind responds to their prodding and is willing to be led indicates that very few of us, however much we sing the praise of idleness, wish we could win a fortune on the pools and never work again, or are convinced that most other people—never ourselves— are bone selfish, do not desire to be associated with an objective that is hard to attain and worth attaining.

Ought it not therefore to be part of the service of the Church to this generation to proclaim the urgency and value of the alternative? We debate much among ourselves about the Christian attitude to war. Most of our complex and necessary debating seems to be directed to the diminution of the horror of war, to the limitation of armaments, and to the duty of a Christian in time of war. There could be a new reality in the debate if we stopped concentrating on the evil of war as a 'thing in itself', and began to relate it to a viable alternative. If I had reluctantly proved to my own satisfaction that we had left the effort too late and had missed our chance, I would still feel it a Christian duty to do all we can to ameliorate the misery of our fellow men. But if, as I do believe, there is still time, though there is little left for further delay, I would feel it a Christian imperative.

9

AFTER THE TAKE-OFF

THE arguments in favour of an intensive Christian campaign to direct the energies of men against the entrenched
evils of poverty and hunger seem overwhelming, but there
is still a dark shadow of doubt. If all the difficulties are
overcome and the ball is set rolling, how fast will it roll
and in which direction? Might it not be that, in spite of all
our good intentions, the second state will be so much worse
than the first that it would have been better never to have
started?

I am profoundly suspicious of hesitation to act that is
based on fears deduced from a long chain of speculative
reasoning. Intelligent prudence is one thing, but a timorous
refusal to move one step until the entire journey has been
mapped in detail is something very different. It is, in fact,
a foolish enterprise to try to draw such a map. The Communists tried it, and ever since have been revising the map
and blurring the details with a fog of words. No obligation
is laid on the Christian to plan with elaborate precision all
the stages of a progress towards a perfect human society.
On the contrary, one of the clearest, if rarely heeded, doc-
trines of Christian theology is that we go one step at a time.
If we have some idea of the general direction in which we
ought to go, and a very definite conviction about the next
immediate step to be taken, the obligation that is laid on us
is to take that step in faith, knowing that until we have
taken it the step that is to follow will not be revealed.

The times of our ignorance that God winked at are
ended. We know about the need of our fellows, and we
know that their need can be met. My own conviction about

that next step is quite clear. But, to test the conviction from another angle, and in deference to those who are less optimistic, or less rash, it could be a useful exercise to examine the reasonably probable and fairly immediate consequences —with the due warning that if the fantastic acceleration of scientific advance is mixed with an internationally directed economic revolution, reasonable probabilities deduced from past experience are very little guide to the future.

If the campaign does come off it will follow the pattern of military enterprise to which it is the alternative. There will be mistakes and failures; the equivalents of the Dardanelles landing and the siege of Monte Cassino. Headlong advances will go too fast, and will have to be pulled back for regrouping. Money and materials will be wasted. The neat and orderly plans emanating from the Geneva and New York HQ will be transmuted into ragged but workable schemes by exasperated, overworked, improvising field officers. It will be messy, confusing, and uneven. But at the end of it there will be a world society, possibly of federal groups, possibly still mainly of independent nations, in which even the most backward will have reached the 200 dollar *per capita* annual income. Every nation will be at the take-off stage of development, with a level sufficiently above subsistence to give a margin for saving, and so for capital investment, and so for accelerating advance.

Advance to what? Beyond any doubt to a Western-type industrialized urban civilization. It makes very little difference whether the development is by centrally directed economic planning on the lines of Moscow or Peking, by the American free-enterprise system, or by the Scandinavian and British compromises. One of the strangest paradoxes of history is that Lenin was captivated by the teachings of Karl Marx. Marx built his doctrine on second-hand observation of the consequences of the Industrial Revolution in England. Marxism is impregnated with the concepts of Western industrial capitalism. If there had been no October Revolution, no Lenin, and no Stalin, Russia would have

Westernized, though probably more slowly. But there was a Lenin, and he became the tutor of Mao-Tse-Tung—and so the government of the People's Republic, though it would hate to be told so, is Westernizing China from within with furious and dedicated activity. The experts smile condescendingly, and tell us that China invariably absorbs and digests her conquerors, and that the Communists will go the way of all who have preceded them. If all that they mean is that the rigid Communist orthodoxy will change out of all recognition with the passing years, they are undoubtedly right. But if they are suggesting that China can transform herself into a prosperous industrial nation and yet remain basically an unchanged society, they underestimate the power of the machine.

The newly independent nations of Asia, Africa, and the Caribbean are headed in the same direction. Their leaders are stepping into the shoes of the departed colonial administrators and, though they wear them with a difference, they are the same shoes. The élite have been trained in the methods of the West in Mission schools or foreign universities, trained in the ways of America or Britain or France or Portugal or Holland or Russia or China, which are Western ways. To maintain the apparatus of State and the prestige of leadership they must obviously supplant those they have driven out or persuaded to depart. They might in a generation or two have developed a new and indigenous type of national society—but not if they are set on raising the living standards of their people. Prosperity in the contemporary world, and the world of the immediate tomorrow, depends on science, technology and industry; and these three create a recognizably uniform social pattern.

Even superficial differences will be minimized. For one thing, the necessity for intensive and continuous international co-operation will destroy the regional isolation that fosters distinctive peculiarity. For another, the inevitable growth in rapid world-wide communication, in news and entertainment, will impress a common culture. To

Third Programme fans the thought of global television shows beamed from orbiting satellites may give no thrill of anticipatory delight, but it is a reasonable assumption that they will both create and distribute a globally acceptable and globally uniform mass culture. The process is already operating. New housing estates in the industrial areas of Vancouver, Scunthorpe, Jamaica or Kenya are virtually identical. So are the advertisements, the radio programmes, the films, and the paperbacks. The well-fed world will incline to monotony. Holiday enclaves and national parks will no doubt be preserved. Thousands of local national equivalents of Bardic crowns and pennillion singing will be supported with nostalgic patriotic fervour. But it will be one world, sharing in or moving to the conditions and values of Detroit or Tokyo.

It will be a world at the same time more comfortable and more alien. It will be more positively peaceful, because that is a necessary prerequisite of the breakthrough to prosperity. It will be politically more stable, for the economic development will create a stabilizing and influential middle class of managers and technicians and scientific farmers. It will open broad roads of social advance to the tough, the clever, and the supple. It will thrust tens of millions of ordinary people into bewildering situations. The progress that snaps the chains of poverty will destroy also the social security of immemorial custom and tradition.

It is probable that the tremendous demand for goods and services liberated by the approach to affluence of all the world will keep all the new industrial workers busily and gainfully employed; probable but not certain. Automation, the application of labour-saving, self-regulating, electronically controlled machinery, will come early to the new factories; and when the miracles of modern science get to work on the factory floor the floor is soon swept clear of humans. My own guess is that the sheer volume and variety of hitherto unmet need in a spectacularly expanding market would be big enough to hold at bay the fearful menace of involuntary leisure until AD 2000, and even to push further into the future its now threatening imminence in the economically advanced nations. The complications of an economy in which supply outruns demand may not hit the human race until well into the twenty-first century. If the adjectives appear to be very oddly chosen to apply to the prospect of leisure, bear in mind that by the efficient application of fully automated production all the potential demand could be supplied by a maximum working week of twenty hours—which leaves a terrible lot of time to kill for those without the inner resources to use time.

But, pushing aside that particular problem, what we could expect to find by the end of the century is a worldwide Western urban industrial society composed for the most part of people to whom moderate affluence will be a new thing. They will embrace the values of Western society. They will want to buy the things we buy. The rising standard of living in Britain and West Germany, for example, has just about reached the pre-war level of the United States. The pattern of spending in Britain and West Germany almost exactly reproduces the pre-war pattern of the United States. It is as though every income level had its own inevitable expenditure pattern. Twenty years on—still on the highly speculative assumption that we don't blow the world to bits and drive the unhappy survivors back to barbarism—Britain will be where America is now. Forty years on India and China and Brazil will be where Britain is now. And how we regard that depends on our opinion of the quality of life in the 'affluent society'.

In the depression years between the world wars the message of the social prophets, inside the Church and outside, was about the corroding evil of unemployment, the need for a planned economy, the virtues of a Welfare State in which the community would accept responsibility for the poor and the ill. My own denomination approved in those years a deeply moving Declaration on a Christian View of Industry, burning with compassion for the suffering of the unemployed. The Declaration has had to be re-written; not only because Britain has had full employment since the end of the war but also because we have discovered that full employment brought with it unsuspected problems.

We thought that poverty was the major cause of crime and delinquency. We find that with less poverty there is more crime. My first ministerial appointment was to a dockland area of intense unemployment. Much of our time in those days was given to trying to help youngsters who had got into scrapes because they had no money. Thirty years later I went back for Anniversary services. The young minister told me that he spent much of his time trying to help youngsters who landed in trouble because they had too much money. One of the wholly unexpected consequences of prosperity is that prisoners are sleeping three in a cell. There are too many of them today for the available accommodation.

The most prosperous countries have the highest suicide rates and the greatest incidence of alcoholism. Physical needs are met and the killer diseases held at bay, but the proportion of the ill is rising. More than half the hospital beds in England are for the mentally sick. Inconspicuous in single rooms in the asphalt jungles of the cities are tens of thousands of lonely and friendless people, enduring an unnatural existence never known in the gregarious family and kinship life of poor but neighbourly communities. Two contemporary sociological surveys out of every three contrast the security and belongingness of the slums that are being demolished with the crippling insecurity and isolation of the new estates that are being built.

The comprehensive criticism of the civilization of the affluent society is too familiar to need any amplification. But before we draw the conclusion that the kindest thing we could do for the hungry poor, in their own best interest, would be to leave them undisturbed in their chummy poverty, we had better look again at our own situation. It is fashionable to be loftily superior about affluence, but do we really believe that England would be a happier and healthier nation if we re-created the squalor of the slums and restored the penury? People who have a little spare money in their pockets for the first time will probably spend it unwisely. Until quite recent times working people in Britain used to pay twopence a week to the insurance man or to the friendly society to make sure of a respectable funeral. The lucky ones with steady jobs saved a little only if they cut down on comforts and economized on necessities. Is it any wonder that the first generation that has not had to look twice at every penny should spend immaturely? Even more to the point, is it any wonder that the descendants of the penniless or of the careful savers alike should think that wealth was the way to happiness?

It is perfectly true that a family can possess a trim modern semi-detached, a car, a television set, a spin-drier, a refrigerator, and a contraption that sounds the alarm and makes the tea in the morning, and still be miserable. But this is a truth to be experienced before it is accepted. The poor are quite sure that they would be happier if they had steak and chips rather than bread and margarine; happier having a holiday on the Costa Brava or at Butlin's than a week with Aunt Ethel in Grimsby. Only by personal experience can they discover that the novelty wears off, that the higher living standards come to be regarded as normal, and that the good life (the 'good time') is still eluding them.

The first generation of an affluent society—which is a quite new phenonomen in human history—is the first total group to be exposed to this unwelcome truth. It could mean that a wholly new opportunity is being given to persuade the human being, who learns only by experience and then reluctantly, to start thinking again about 'living standards'. When that which for so long appeared utterly unattainable has at last been attained, and still does not satisfy, a new direction may be reconnoitred. It will not be a return to bread and margarine—or to cheap rice or mealic maize. It may be a search for a 'standard of living'.

That could be wishful thinking on my part, but at least I am sure that the cramping, distorting pressures of involuntary poverty cannot be commended as better than the dangers of decent living. Nor will the hungry now be persuaded to stay hungry and like it. In his fascinating and informative study of the attempts of the Churches to influence and capture the working-classes in Victorian England, Professor Inglis concludes that they never had much hope of success. When the workers pictured a better life, they pictured it in terms of wages, working conditions, and housing conditions. They turned to politics and to trade union organization. They have secured most of what they wanted. The labouring poor of such countries as Kenya and British Guiana have seen the same picture, and are setting off on the same road. They may not get what they want, but if they do—which is the assumption of this chapter—they may find themselves in AD 2000 in the peculiar mental state of the British or American or Swedish worker in AD 1964; loyal to the union, but with no longer a crusading zeal, sceptical and unexcited about politics. Like the depressing university students recently interviewed by Dr Zweig they may be almost wholly absorbed in the pursuit of personal material security.

But because man is man, a strange being haunted by dreams of paradise and echoes of immortality, this state, however prolonged, can only be transitional. Man cannot live by bread alone. The message may be too hard to bear when he has no bread, except perhaps as a consolation for an empty belly and a dying child. The understanding of its real meaning becomes possible when he has bread to spare.

So I come back to the query with which this chapter opened. The anxieties and doubts about the quality of life in an economically accelerating industrial urban society are well founded, but are anxieties which should serve as a guide to the desirable future development of this type of society. They do not justify the romanticization of hunger, poverty and disease. They warn us that an annual income per head of two hundred dollars, or of two thousand, is not the final goal of human striving. And as the developing nations, whatever they may say and sincerely believe about preserving the values of their own disintegrating cultures, will inexorably be drawn to the values of Western civilization and will seek after its standards, what happens to them after the take-off depends on the values and standards by which in the next forty years the West chooses to live.

10

STANDARDS OF LIVING

WHEN we consider the essential physical needs of a human being we know, more or less, where we are. As we saw, there is room for argument about calorie intake and protein deficiency, but the argument moves within reasonably precise statistical limits. When the nutritional experts have finished with their slide-rules we know that the upper and lower limits are 3000 and 2000 calories respectively. But when the basic needs have been met, and we look at what does happen, or should happen, next, and why, we move from the fairly firm ground of biology to the cloudy upper air of social psychology.

What the economist means by a higher standard of living is a wider range of goods and services and an effective consumer demand that can make use of them. A wider range of possibilities involves a wider range of choice. The under-nourished poor peasant has virtually two choices only; to have his cheap rice or to go without. The suburban housewife wanders with a shopping list through the supermarket, exercising her choice among a bewildering variety of alternatives. She is not primarily concerned with deciding whether her family shall eat or go hungry, but with a balance of much more complex assessments. She had beef over the week-end, and sausages yesterday. Smoked haddock would make a nice change, but she will have to watch what she spends if she is to squeeze the nylons she wants out of the housekeeping money, so perhaps it had better be fish fingers. Peas go well with fish fingers. Shall she stick to X's Utopian tinned peas she usually buys, or try those Y's Arcadian tinned peas she saw on television the other night?

Wider range of choice means a continuous series of decisions that are not compelled by necessity. The decisions flow from states of mind, from judgements, probably not lucid and deliberately organized but none the less effective, about the quality of the good life. The earlier part of this study dealt with the technical problem of fuelling the human machine. The unflattering description served its purpose in focussing attention on the extent and gravity of the purely physical problem, but, even on that coldly utilitarian level it was obvious that fuelling was not an end in itself. As soon as the problem is solved in any society, a much more important question arises. When the machine is in fully efficient working order, what is it supposed to do? When the machine is also the mechanic, how does it in fact determine its own purpose?

There are two ways of tackling this question, both of them valid. One is to attempt to deduce from first principles —Christian theology, or dialectical materialism, or social engineering—the nature of an ideal society, and then to devise incentives and discouragements that will guide men and women in the required direction. The other, which is the method that I have so far used and propose to continue, is to try to find out the way they took when they got the chance, and to see where that path leads.

The first, obvious point to note is that, when the stable pattern imposed by poverty and necessity is broken, the concept of a standard of living is subject to continuous change. It is not merely that people have in large measure what they used to have in small. The man who had to exist on two modest daily meals of maize does not for long rest content with six large daily meals of maize. He may stick to maize as the staff of life for the rest of his days, but he likes a change as well. He discovers, or is more probably taught by his wife, that wants always increase just a little faster than the means for gratifying them. What used to be comforts become necessities, and what used to be luxuries become comforts, and in due course the luxuries that became comforts become necessities.

One purely objective reason is that the capacity of the human stomach is limited. In desperate poverty almost the whole of a meagre income has to go on food. As the pressure eases, the proportion remains high to secure adequate food. But as it continues to ease, the amount spent rises slowly but the proportion falls. By the beginning of this century, when Britain was well clear of her take-off, having many poor but few at the level of subsistence, the proportion of income spent on food was about thirty per cent. During the whole of the century it has stayed on that mark with very little variation, which may indicate—for American and Scandinavian statistics show the same pattern— that when economic advance is well under way one-third of income is enough to meet essential needs.

In fact, if one gives a very strict definition to 'essential' a considerably smaller proportion would be enough. The percentage has remained constant because there has been a steady transference to more varied and more expensive foods. Carbohydrates are giving place to proteins. We are eating less potatoes and bread, more meat and eggs and milk. Smaller joints of better meat are fashionable. More poultry is being eaten. Consumption of fruit is rising rapidly. And what have been called recreational foods, such as fancy biscuits and ice-cream, are now part of our regular diet. There are even signs that the long reign of 'chips with everything' is beginning to wane. Almost incredibly, more and more of the English are enjoying their food and starting to be fussy about it.

Where, then, is proportionate expenditure increasing? Not, surprisingly, on housing or fuel, though if the sharp rise in the price of land and the trend to house ownership continue, getting a roof over one's head may take a bigger slice out of the wage packet. Not, despite the warnings of the moralists, on drink or tobacco. As one who has fre-

D

quently moralized on this particular theme I would still contend that we spend far more on them than is good for us, but the fact is that proportionate expenditure has declined. The main increase is in labour-saving domestic gadgets; then on cars, cameras, record-players and records, tape-recorders, foreign travel, cosmetics and toilet articles. Women led the way on the last two, but the men are catching up fast.

The new pattern is reflected in a new attitude to possessions. When things like furniture and clothes have to be bought from the small surplus remaining when the daily necessities have been secured, they are made to last. A table would be expected to endure for a life-time, a Sunday suit to give ten years of careful wear before being relegated to the lowlier status of a working suit, shoes to last with regular repairing for five or six years. The diminution of this expectation or desire is an overt sign of a more sophisticated society. Women lead the way in this too. Perfectly good hats are discarded because they are out of style, make the wearers feel dowdy, and provide no more the satisfaction they gave a few months earlier. Clothes are scrapped long before they are worn out. Shoes and shirts are no longer carefully repaired, but are handed to the local Steptoe. The outstanding illustration is the car. New and slightly varied models are issued with a great fanfare every year.

There is a trace of utilitarian reason in this. As industrialization develops the cost of labour increases, so that, for example, it is less expensive to hire a television set for a week than to employ a gardener for four hours a week. Repairing, which is mainly personal service, gets more and more costly. It can be cheaper to buy a new car or a new electric blanket than to pay for the continual repair of an old one, or at least there is not enough in it to inhibit the purchase of the new. But utility is not a dominant reason. Acceptance of obsolescence is a psychological adaptation to the fact of a changing society. It is also, which is not a bad thing, a sign of growing readiness to experiment, to try out new possessions to see if they satisfy an inner need and to dispose of them if they fail to do so or if the first satisfaction fades.

Obsolescence, in fact, is an economic and psychological necessity for a materially progressive society. I used to think that it was an evil peculiar to the salesmanship drives of capitalist industry. I am not so sure now that it is an evil, and it is evident from contemporary Soviet developments that it is not confined to capitalism. It may be argued that the restless changes in fashion are no more than continuous transitions to an undiscovered destination, but it could be that in them is the first faint foreshadowing of a healthy sitting loose to possessions.

The second feature of the changed pattern of living is that a great deal more time is available for leisure. The days of manual toil from dawn till dusk, broken by occasional feast days, give place to the five-day forty-hour week with paid holidays. The change has never so far come without a bitter industrial struggle, but, on the long view of social history, it seems to be an irresistible process. The point comes at which organized labour sees greater benefit in more free time than in more money, and at which the development of mechanized industry and production techniques make labour costs marginal in total costs and so permit the reduction in working hours. The point, indeed, may be coming at which fully automated industry will demand a working week much shorter than the worker will cheerfully accept.

Oddly enough, there is just now in both Britain and America a curious resistance to additional leisure. Since the end of the war the demand for a shorter working week has really been a demand for more overtime payment. The theoretic and contractual working week in this country has declined from 47·5 to 42 hours: the actual working week has increased from 45·4 to 46·7 hours. The latter figure may be a considerable under-estimate. More and more typists doing a five-day week spend Saturday serving in shops and supermarkets. We all know somebody who will do a little painting and decorating in his spare time, for a consideration. And if we add in all the 'do-it-yourself' activity, which begins as a hobby and ends as work, the total of working hour bumps up dramatically. One of the great discoveries of our generation, and one not so wittily absurd as at first sight it appears, is Parkinson's Law, that work expands in proportion to the number of people available to do it. It has been quite seriously suggested that highly industrialized society subconsciously creates unnecessary paper work in order to stave off the hideous prospect of leisure. It is certainly true that the new buildings which dominate our cities are nearly all offices.

But the real reason for the halt is that in the continual tension between the desire for more free time and the desire for the possessions that mark a higher standard of living, the second is pulling more strongly. Hire-purchase has put within tempting reach desirable and expensive commodities that might otherwise not have been saved for, but which have to be paid for month by month once the contract is signed and the goods are installed. Ronald Brech, in *Britain 1984*, the statistical, forecasting counterblast to George Orwell he prepared for Unilever, argues that the demand is now concentrating on machinery that will lift the burden of drudgery from the home, and that the demand for leisure has become a demand for more concentrated time off; two days at the week-end and a long summer holiday. He anticipates that by 1984 the official working week may have diminished to four days and the paid holidays expanded to a month, but that the actual working time will be much what it is now.

He may be right, but my own guess is that before very long the time spent at work will begin to shrink again. Like the human stomach, the capacity of the kitchen is limited. A man—or more likely a man and his wife—with a good basic wage will work overtime for a refrigerator, or electric mixer, a deep freeze, an automatic polisher, and so on, but once they have them will feel no compulsive urgency to work for two of each. Nevertheless, even if Mr Brech is the more reliable prophet, there is no disputing the fact that, compared with subsistence existence, a higher standard of living carries with it increased leisure.

Those who looked forward to this day a hundred years ago rejoiced in the prospect, fondly anticipating that it would provide increased opportunity for culture and for practice of the gracious arts of civilization. But the liberated artisan has not made a bee-line for the museums and art galleries, or devoted his free Saturdays to the study of philosophy. His needs have been supplied by commercial entertainment. For more than forty years the fantasy world of the cinema gave him something to look at that would pass the time without straining his intelligence. The opulent, glittering, insubstantial empire collapsed when a smaller screen brought the soporific into his own home. The empty cinemas have become the Bingo Halls, temples devoted to the most moronic craze ever devised to kill time. People with money in their pockets and time on their hands needed antidotes to boredom, and they got them: streamlined professional football, greyhound racing, wrestling, pop-singing groups, and a host of other spectacles to be watched.

The sad indictment of wasted time and wasted wealth flows easily; a little too easily to be wholly justified. We need to remember again that this is the first time that the majority of a generation have had both time and money at their disposal. They had little preparation or education for it, possibly because nobody expected it quite so soon. It takes time to learn how to use time, and twenty years of moderate affluence is not a terribly long time. The critics expect too much too soon, and paint far too lurid a picture of the feckless, improvident masses.

The popularity of undemanding escape entertainment is not solely due to widespread soggy stupidity. The time and motion study men, the efficiency experts, and the productivity drivers have stepped up the tempo of industrial and commercial life. An eight-hour working day at modern pressure induces real mental fatigue, for which Coronation Street is a better cure than King Lear. Even so, as the resilient human organism begins to adapt to the new situation, a growing minority is nibbling tentatively at King Lear. Sales of pop discs are astronomical, but sales of classical records climb steadily. Ballet is becoming popular. The football fans are no longer regulars. They want good football, and stay away if it is not provided. The sport that is growing fastest is the active sport of sailing. Enrolments in voluntary evening classes increase year by year. Men go out shopping with their wives on Saturdays, and are taking to the feminine art of comparing prices and qualities like ducks to water. Young couples, decorating their own homes, do a lot of serious thinking about designs and styles and colours. All these are as yet but minority movements, but they are the movements of the leaders, the Joneses with whom the neighbours keep up, the leaven in the Bingo lump.

The emphasis, whether one is in an armchair before the television set or contending with the winds and tides in a small boat, is on personal and self-centred enjoyment. Is this surprising? The industrial city is a man-made environment, knowing next to nothing about the alternation of the seasons and nothing at all about seed-time and harvest. The rhythm of the annual cycles of labour in the fields, with its high days and festivals, gave a social structure to leisure. The city leaves men and women to their own devices. Those who save a little escape to the suburbs, to better houses and bigger gardens and no sense of belonging to a community. Life is centred on the home and family. The typical example of the higher standard of living in contemporary Britain is a house in a new estate in a town in the Black Country or West Riding. Within it is spotless, bright, well-furnished and comfortable; a source of pride to its owners. Outside are the endless, indistinguishable streets, the dirt and grime, the scarred dumping grounds and slag-heaps and mill chimneys of industry. The picture is one of private affluence in public squalor, of which the inward-looking self-regarding family is both the cause and the effect.

There are welcome signs of change. We are not as indifferent as we used to be to civic dirt and ugliness. Slum clearance schemes, and the demolition of Victorian city centres which is compelled by the torrent of road traffic give an opportunity for the creation of deliberately designed beauty, and the opportunity is sometimes taken. But not often. The meaning, so far, of the higher standard is expressed in the gadget-filled, well furnished West Riding house, with a car in the garage, roses in the front garden, a fur coat in the wardrobe and a pantry stacked with tinned food.

Criticism is easy. The affluent are trying to buy satisfaction and are failing. They have filled the beneficent contemplative rest of leisure with a thousand distractions, so that it becomes more exhausting than work. But criticism can wait. Let us ask first why this way of life is the end product of the escape from indigence.

There are two obvious and straightforward reasons. The first is that when people have been compelled to go without material comforts, or to get a few by dint of sacrificial saving, comforts are irresistibly attractive. No-one has any natural affection for a bumpy mattress or frayed linoleum or cold bedrooms. If the psychological benefit of material possessions is exaggerated, the exaggeration is a consequence of deprivation. The second reason is that people have to prove to themselves that they really are moving to a higher standard. So they look at what people do on the social level just above them and, tentatively at first and then with growing confidence, they begin to follow suit.

A good deal has been written, particularly by American sociologists, of the prestige value of possessions and their use as overt demonstration of social grade. A mink coat, so they say, is no warmer than a coney-skin, but to have one is a sign to the world—and to yourself—that you have arrived at the top. A young executive must be neatly clothed, freshly laundered, and trimly barbered. The cut of his coat and the size of his car proclaim that he is, for all to note, a young executive. The sociologists relate this to a conformity induced by a basic insecurity, an artificial attempt to re-capture in a rapidly changing society the security that came from stability. Even the vanishing race of beatniks were rigidly conventional in their sartorial nonconformity. Only the very rich or the very eccentric can really please them-selves.

The pattern of living adopted by the newly affluent is, then, to a considerable degree their affirmation to them-selves and to others that they have attained a higher social level. In order that the affirmation may be recognizable it must conform to a generally accepted pattern, which brings us to the contemporary paradox of atomistic family units that are socially conformist. Each unit is primarily con-cerned with its own satisfactions and enjoyments, but seeks to find them just as all the others do. Pastel shades for front door colours are 'in', and almost overnight a street of dark green and dark brown doors burst into the pastel variety of a self-consciously refined rainbow. Knee-length boots, cape coats and fur hats are 'in', so that all England looks as though it had been invaded by female Cossacks. Possibly by the time this is in print wedge shoes and tweed suits and sensible hats will be the compulsory wear of the fashion conscious, and all England will look like a grand re-union at a County point-to-point.

How does this knowledge of what is expected at the social level of affluence spread so quickly? And is it really true that, unlike the rich or the eccentric, people are spend-ing their additional time and money not to please themselves but to satisfy a concept of what they feel they ought to enjoy? Is the whole idea of the desirable standard of living, at this level, determined in fact by the persistent pressure of advertising?

11

THE SELLERS OF DREAMS

ONE of the chapters in Professor J. K. Galbraith's book *American Capitalism* examines advertising as a facet of the opulent society of the United States, and makes its provocative points by direct contrast with the situation in underdeveloped countries. Professor Galbraith is not one of the most fervent admirers of the advertising industry. It would be a crude simplification, but not a travesty of his argument, to say that he regards it as very largely a social and economic waste, as the spending of vast sums to persuade people to buy things they could very well do without.

It is not necessary, he asserts, to advertise the things that people cannot do without. No bright boy in a Madison Avenue Agency has to think up a catchy slogan to persuade a hungry man to buy bread, but teams of bright boys have to work hard to convince the well-fed American to buy one particular brand of cigarettes or toothpaste when a dozen competing brands are almost wholly identical. Persuasion only begins to count when the marginal utility of money is low, when purchases are casual and not the final stages of long and careful calculation.

Professor Galbraith is not angry about advertising. He is ruefully amused; amused that packaging and sales talk sells softened, bleached, tasteless bread, that the selling point for breakfast cereals is the noise they make and not their food value; amused at the economists who do get angry about advertising costs, not realizing that the rules of their nineteenth century economics of scarcity do not apply in an economy of plenty. He gives the impression that it is all rather ridiculous, but that the economy can afford it. His purpose is to puncture the pretensions of the solemn high priests of American advertising, and he succeeds by concentrating his fire on the salesmanship of tobacco and alcohol. But he rarely gets far below the surface.

The reader who shares the popular suspicion that the advertisers practise a dangerous and potent art half-way on the road to black magic will not have his fears dispersed by Professor Galbraith's large tolerances. He will still suspect that somehow, by shrewd and subtle pressure, he is being manipulated. Part of the difficulty is that advertising has a twofold purpose and that the two aims overlap. One, which takes up a much greater proportion of the total than is generally recognized, is the simple giving of information. The announcement of an orchestral concert, the items, the players, the conductor, the price of seats, and the time and place, is an advertisement. The church notice board is an advertisement. The colour plate in a glossy magazine, showing a carpet and giving its name, size and price, is an advertisement.

There can surely be no doubt that advertising in this sense performs an essential service in a complex modern society. To protect the customer, the information given should be accurate, and there should be enough of it to enable him to come to an intelligent decision, but if this is so his choice is his own. It is when persuasion is added to announcement that we smell, or think we smell, the odour of witchcraft.

There is, of course, nothing inherently wrong about persuasion. If there is, all preachers should stop preaching and the SCM Press ought to close down immediately. The suspicion about advertising is that its persuasion is not by rational argument but by skilled suggestion. The commodity to be sold is associated with a desirable state, whether there is any logical connection or not. Indeed, some students of the market research, motivation research, product research and copy research that clutter the industry have come very close to declaring that the advertisers are selling qualities of life and tagging on commodities as part of a package deal.

Spine-chilling stories of powerful and unscrupulous 'hidden persuaders' should be taken with a grain of salt. On investigation, the classical examples of products swept to fame and profit by cunning campaigns—a dog food, a cereal, packed raisins—prove to have been good products brought to the notice of a wider constituency; information more than persuasion. The campaigns that fall flat, and there are many, are not remembered. A man can be persuaded that he has a want he had not realized before, or that a particular article will satisfy a known want, but he cannot be persuaded by the most brilliant copy writer that he wants what he knows he doesn't want.

It is where the reality of a new want has to be established, or where there is competition between virtually identical commodities, that the technique of persuasion by association finds its effective field of operation. Well centred in the advertisement for a medium priced car is an elegant and most attractive young woman. There is no explicit condition that one has to have such a young woman before being allowed to buy the car. The implication is that, if one is the sort of young man likely to be associated with such charming females, this is the appropriate car to own. The tinned soup served by the duchess draws well-bred approval from her immaculate dinner party. Distinguished old gentlemen and virile young gentlemen, chic ladies of leisure and impossibly neat housewives commend by their presence in the picture whiskies and wrist-watches, sink-units and biscuits and china. They look dignified, poised, efficient, confident and healthy.

The selling point is most often the tacit assumption that if I, the potential customer, want to justify the feeling that I am essentially that sort of person, this is the soap or wallpaper that I ought to have. Only very rarely, in the case of cosmetics or perfumes, is there the hint of a promise that it will transform me into the sort of person I want to be. Sometimes the line is that without the product I will be out of step with all my more intelligent contemporaries. Sometimes, as with deodorants, it is a sympathetic warning that thoughtless carelessness is holding me back from the social success that would otherwise be mine.

There is continuous criticism of the content of particular advertisements, especially of those which by a careful choice of words tell the truth but not the whole truth and so mislead. This is an eminently useful operation, but it should not be confused with the criticism that the advertisers are impressing on the public mind a deplorably low social ideal. The argument of this second criticism is that the advertisers, employing with relentless persistence subtly modulated variations on the themes of fear and greed and social embarrassment, of social conformity and longing for romance or fame, are for coldly calculated commercial ends creating the image of the desirable *persona*.

The argument exaggerates the skill of the agencies and underestimates the intelligence of the customers. The element of justification for it is that particular emotional needs are isolated, the appetites titillated, and the balance of personal values distorted. But I have very little doubt that the ones who are most successful in the business are those who know, by flair or by consumer research, what the public wants. Those who got above themselves and fancied their skill at driving the sheep-like masses—as when they thought they could put women back into hobble skirts—found themselves marching briskly alone. The fifty-year old gentleman with an expanding waistline and a tendency to puff when climbing stairs buys a fancy waistcoat and a Tyrolean hat because they make him feel youthful and dashing. The advertisers cash in on it with exotic backgrounds and pictures of slim fifty year olds looking like Rex Harrison and wearing fancy waistcoats and Tyrolean hats; but they do not create the middle-aged nostalgia for youth.

In short, advertising very efficiently communicates information to individuals in a well-to-do but loose-knit society, and accurately mirrors the aspirations and desires of the public to whom it communicates. The picture that is mirrored is not, in my judgement, as deplorable as the more disapproving critics imply. It is confused, but the confusion arises from the conflict of desires in the human mind. It shows people who want to look sufficiently like their neighbours to feel socially secure, and yet sufficiently different to feel that they are distinct persons. They want to be liked, admired and envied. They want to be comfortable and safe, and yet to feel that life is adventurous and exciting. They want to holiday in Spain, but to have tea and steak and chips when they get there. They want their children to do better than themselves. They want to daydream of sudden fortune and improbable romance, knowing perfectly well that they are daydreaming.

The social context is new, but when these bits and pieces I have collected from the advertisers' case-books are fitted together, the result is strangely familiar. Translated into terms appropriate to the age, this is what men and women wanted to be like in Chaucerian England or New Testament Palestine. The difference, and this is where the tributary rejoins the main stream of the preceding chapter, is that when the prison gates of poverty are opened people are able at last to go into the markets to buy the things that they think will satisfy their desires.

The point to be emphasized is that the contemporary picture does not show a tragic moral decline or cultural degradation. Dr J. A. C. Brown hits the nail squarely on the head in the concluding chapter of *Techniques of Persuasion*. 'The picture presented by some members of the Pilkington Committee and by such writers as Raymond Williams or F. R. Leavis and Denys Thompson of a once sturdy and self-reliant peasantry living in an "organic" society with their genuine folk-arts, or of industrial workers who at a later period had a warm and cosy working-class culture worthy of preservation, both now perverted by a mean, money-grubbing, and ignorant élite which has "brainwashed" them into accepting Western films when what they "really" want is Shakespeare and John Bunyan, is ludicrous when translated into the terms of modern realities.'

Neither, to be candid, does the pattern of contemporary desires show that economic ease has brought a splendid moral revival or a cultural renaissance. But these are early days. And the picture is changing. When he was Minister of Education, Lord Eccles observed: 'The parents whose children are now beginning to reach our schools are those who were the first in their families to have secondary education. They know what education is, and what it can do for their children. They will ask for it for their children—and they will know what to ask for.' He was over-optimistic, but on the right track. One of the most encouraging aspects of Britain today is that education is being taken seriously. It is taken for granted that it deserves a high priority in national expenditure. More and more working class families are prepared to encourage their children to go to universities.

A university course does not automatically guarantee moral perfection or cultural virtuosity, but it can widen and deepen appreciation of the possibilities of life; and one by-product of the affluent society is that increasing numbers of young people are being exposed to these possibilities. It would be ridiculous to expect an instantaneous and comprehensive change in the accepted scale of values, but it would be unduly cynical to expect no change.

It is, however, realistic to expect that as comfort becomes more of a norm and less of a novelty there will be a growing sense of disappointment at the quality of life. It will be discovered that the markets can supply the material wants but cannot give the satisfactions that the deprived imagined them to embody. Where we go from there is uncertain. It may be to the artificially induced stimulation of jaded minds: to drugs and sick jokes and pornography and spectacles of violence, increasing the dose to get a sufficient reaction. Or it may be to the recognition that man is a creature so made that he finds enduring satisfaction only in the adventures of the mind and the quests of the spirit.

I am not arguing that the second course is the more immediately probable, though the conjunction of greater leisure, better education, and wider opportunities is in its favour. The direction of a peaceful and prosperous world society will depend, in part, on the wisdom of its educators. It will depend even more, I believe, on the quality of the witness made by Christian people to the enduring and ultimate values. A Church that is wholly accommodated to the world, and that ceases to remind sinful and selfish man that he is called to be a little lower than the angels and the heir of an everlasting kingdom, will have thrown away a new and tremendous opportunity to serve the redemptive purposes of God.

If the opportunity is taken it could be, that in a world where none need lack material necessities and reasonable comforts, the desires of men would to their great good be concentrated more on the standard of living and less on living standards. But the main point I want to make is that the first and worse course of the alternatives is not inevitable. There is no reason to believe that the conquest of hunger and poverty will release men from physical affliction only to imprison them more dreadfully in moral degradation. To hold back from the call of mercy and compassion because of such speculative fear is like refraining from walking along an appointed road lest there be lions in the way around the corner.

12

A CHRISTIAN IMPERATIVE

I T is impossible to stand completely outside the society in which we are involved, and to analyse wholly impartially the constitution of contemporary attitudes, but the attempt to get somewhere near to it must be made if this study is to end as realistically as it began. I make the attempt by asking yet another question. Is a crusade for higher living standards really the business of the Church, as the last chapter suggested, or something better left to the economist, the nutritional scientist, and the social engineer?

The snap answer is that Christians can be economists and scientists, but this evades the real and serious point. One of the key words of today is 'belonging'. All over the place, in technical journals on personnel management as in appeals for community centres, there is emphasis on the human need to belong. We have had so many violent upheavals that we have become transient and rootless, and there is no sustaining life in rootlessness. We must put down roots before it is too late so that we may begin to live. There is a strong, sweet sense of security in a firm relationship to a social group.

We can see this idea working itself out most clearly in the new science of human relations within industry. The basic assumption is that industrial conflict comes from a misunderstanding or misuse of the social system within industry; that if management can clear the lines of communication, can realize that the system is an integral unity, and can so explain this to the workers that they in turn will understand, the conflict will wither away. An unofficial strike, for example, following a row over wash-basins, really had nothing to do with wash-basins. They just sparked off a conflict caused by the deep resentment of the workers at being treated as of so little account that they were not even consulted when a more effective and efficient rearrangement of shift work was brought into operation. If only they had been treated as human beings there would have been no trouble. They want to belong, and they cannot belong unless they feel part of the team.

'Team' is another key word. Underlying it is the idea that in all human organizations the whole is greater than the sum of the parts. Industry used to need hard driving leaders because it knew no other way of getting things done. The correct and more scientific way, or so it is now argued, is through harmonious group morale. Somehow or other we must adjust our human relations so that the group works together, and then all will be well.

The expert would sniff disdainfully at that 'somehow or other'. The tensions that disrupt social harmony must be eased away by the impersonal and impartial application of scientific method. Physical science has enabled man to master and control his physical environment. The same techniques can develop a 'science of man' which will give us the same mastery over our social environment. Science, inevitably, means scientists. The integrating of groups and the promotion of psychological harmony are skilled and expert jobs. Hence the newly risen and swelling corps of personnel managers, public relations officers, industrial psychologists, non-directive counsellors, and the like.

It is fully understandable that in the storms and stresses of our time men should desire a haven of peace. It is understandable too that having gained a large measure of social security they should want to establish it firmly. It is undeniable that much social conflict is unnecessary, and that a man needs to feel he belongs somewhere. But when all that has been conceded, the fact remains that this pseudo-scientific approach to Utopia is plain crazy. It is much too simple. A worker may be at odds with his foreman or with

the management because he has some nagging inner dis-
harmony that is projected on the nearest apparent object.
But he may dislike the foreman because the foreman is
incompetent or unfair, and may fight the management
because the rates of pay are bad. It is all very well to talk
glibly of resolving conflict through the team spirit, but if
two members of the team have sincere and radically different views about the policy to be followed, no amount of
slushy rhetoric will end the conflict.

All that may happen is that, in the interests of harmony,
both will compromise and each will be dissatisfied. The
social engineers are well aware of this, and bend their
energies now to blending teams of compatibles. The unfortunate thing is that no progress was ever made by such
a group. A happy committee can burnish and refine existing
policies and institutions, and can journey with slow un-
animity along a well-signposted path, but it cannot initiate
or discover. Group argument can squash absurdities and
can, if there is a genuine clash of minds, suggest new
avenues of research or endeavour. But hard and original
thinking has to be done by individuals.

It is perhaps significant that the ideal of the social scientist
is the aim of the physicist; to establish a stable equilibrium.
The trouble is that in human affairs a stable equilibrium is
the harbinger of decay and death. It sounds attractive to be
a member of a predictable and stable society; so attractive
that if the price to be paid is the surrender of individual
freedom the price will be paid, provided that the surrender
is sufficiently eloquently camouflaged. I do not think that
this is an empty fear. Shrewd observers are beginning to
warn us that a disconcerting feature of our present generation is their eagerness to be told. They are not greatly
interested in assessing the sources of authority. The chemical
engineer, the second vice-president, the junior assistant, and
the theological student want it laid on the line for them.

In practice, the fine phrases about group harmony and
the resolution of social conflicts come down to the manipu-

lation and moulding of human personalities to the require-
ments of the machine or the expert. And that is a bad thing.
The non-directive counsellor and the warming-up group
sessions of American big business are the dialectical expert
and the Communist self-criticism class seen in a mirror.

One gets used to the tolerant condescension of the social
scientist as he dismisses the theologian as a fumbling
amateur in the world of reality. But who in fact is the
realist? The real situation is that we are seeing the emer-
gence of yet one more of the attempts to snatch easily and
without pain the good things of the kingdom of God. The
preaching of the social engineers is going down quite well
because it does relate to felt human needs; but it is offering
to the spiritually hungry a tasteless sandwich without nour-
ishment wrapped in a contemporary package. The truth is
that man feels he needs to belong because he is a child of
God who is lost and far from home. It is a good thing to
have a nice house and a full larder, to work in a happy
office or an efficient engineering shop, but the whole needs
of life cannot and should not there be fulfilled.

I am not, I hope, wrecking the whole of my argument in
the last chapter. I am fully convinced that at the heart of
Christian faith is personal response to a personal Saviour,
and that the majestic divine plan of redemption cannot be
confined to material benefit in this mortal life. But I am
equally convinced that the material welfare of mankind is
not outside the plan. Any doctrine which seeks to exalt the
spiritual by condemning the material misconceives both.
Nor am I denying the service to mankind which can and
should be rendered by the economist, the scientist, and the
sociologist. What I am concerned to deny is the absolutizing
of proximate goals. The economists, theorizing too soon,
constructing a pattern of society from a handful of facts,
made that mistake a century and a half ago. The social
scientists are making the same mistake. The future development of human society, and the standards by which it will
choose to live, are hidden in the mists. We shall not reach

journey's end in the next three generations, and it is foolish to expect the stability and security of equilibrium. All we can wisely do is to look for the way of immediate progress that is according to the will of God.

That reflection sounds sadly old-fashioned. Except for the incorrigibly romantic optimist belief in progress died thirty years ago. It would be good for all of us if it revived. Perhaps it died because the 'socially progressive' began marking time instead of going on.

The company of those who look forward rather than back may be divided into three groups—and here I borrow the analysis made by Professor Peter Kuin in his inaugural address when he was installed in the chair of economic and industrial sociology at the University of Amsterdam. The three groups are the awakened, the awakeners, and the critics. The awakened are those who have grim and unpleasant memories of the past, and are doubtful of their present security. In our Western civilization this is the working-class. They still remember unemployment, privation, and underpaid and over-strenuous toil. The days gone by are like a nightmare that may yet return. Their social actions and attitudes are often unconsciously more attuned to a conflict that has ended than to the present, but because they have a compulsive determination never to return to the bondage of the past they look as by instinct to the future.

Generally speaking, they did not awaken themselves. Drudgery and deprivation breed a deadly acceptance. The mental chains of servitude have to be broken before such men will dare to dream and aspire to hope. This was the state of the industrial workers of Britain at the dawn of the nineteenth century. It is the state of the poor of Africa and Asia today. The awakeners, those who have made them aware of their condition and shown a way to rise above it, have more often come from outside their ranks than from within. The awakeners are men like St Francis, who cast his lot by deliberate choice with the poor and dispossessed.

They are the rebel aristocrats who strove against their own kind and on the side of a struggling middle class. They are middle-class stalwarts like the High Tory Oastler or the Communist Engels who were appalled by the misery of the under-privileged. Sometimes they have been driven by frustrated pride, deeming it better to lead their social inferiors than to follow their social equals. Most often they have been men of tender conscience and strong moral sense who had too much intelligence to rest content with personal charity, moved by their outraged sense of justice to social reform. In this group are many Christian leaders, great and small.

The third group are the critics, always uneasy companions. They are the men of quick wit, more often inclined to deflate the pomposity of the governors than to sympathize with the sorrows of the governed. Their weapon is the barbed arrow of ridicule; their talent the fear-inspiring gift of baring in the cold light of reason the snug, smug motives of action. They are welcome allies in the first, odds-against endeavours of a campaign, but are regarded as dubious assets when victory is near or won. They strip the mask of hypocrisy from the face of the wicked dominion of the capitalist, and we applaud, but they seem to have no sense of the respect due to a good, hard-working, Homburg-wearing, brief-case-carrying Trade Union secretary. As likely as not, they will pause in their probing to prick the bubbles of their own complacency. They are exasperating, unbearable, and essential.

The trouble with progress is that it keeps on going. The reformers who raced ahead, and then stayed put, suddenly discover that they have been left behind . . . or, which is worse, are left behind and think that they are still in front. It is the interpretation given to 'social progress' that makes it look so dusty, and provides so easy a target for the cynics. The emotional feel derives, historically, from a mingling of middle-class reformist agitation against privilege and establishment, mainly politically directed, and a working-class reformist agitation against exploitation, mainly industrially directed; a mingling, if not yet a merging, which became explicit in the formation of the Labour party.

Without trying to compile an all-embracing list, I would suggest that the following concepts give a fair impression of what is now regarded as socially progressive. There should be opportunity for education up to the highest level for all those qualified to benefit from it. There should be equality of opportunity in trades and professions. There should be a narrowing of the limits, by taxation at the upper levels and higher wages at the lower, within which incomes vary. There should be social security and protection for the elderly, the handicapped, the poor, and the ill. The pressure of Government should be directly applied to the encouragement of desirable social reforms, and if encouragement is not sufficient (as in the supply of youth agencies) the State should act as sponsor and provider. International co-operation is good. Discriminations based on class or colour of skin are bad. The worker ought to have a larger share of responsibility for the administration of the industry on which his livelihood depends. The profit motive is suspect, and should be replaced by the motive of social service.

Not so long ago that list would have bristled with hair-trigger emotional explosives. It would smell sulphurously of the pit, or shine with the bright glow of a future waiting to be built by dedicated souls. There is no punch in it now. The phrases are used and the ideas faithfully expounded, but they are dulled and worn with use, no longer shining, new-minted coins. Most of the goals have been attained or are so near attainment that urging society towards them is marking time, not making progress.

It is also true that many of them looked much more attractive in the haze of the future than in the chilly light of the present. They were not easily gained. They are the rewards of a gruelling marathon, not a hundred yards' sprint, but those who have inherited the rewards—and never knew the ardour or the heartbreak of the struggle, or the place from which the race began—are not particularly impressed by them. Nationalization was the climax of a bitter political struggle to which ardent reformers devoted themselves for generations, but Lord Robens's miners and Dr Beeching's porters do not think of themselves as those who dwell in the outer courts of Utopia. Socialism has become practical politics, responsible politics, prosaic politics. The progressive has very nearly arrived, and the approaching terminus does not much resemble the picture on the travel brochure.

Probably the greatest disappointment of the advanced progressive, and the biggest single cause of the relapse into cynicism and lethargy, was the failure of the Soviet experiment. A great nation has been created and an empire subdued, but the optimistic dream of a community of brotherhood was brutally shattered. There is today sober and unemotional appraisal of the possibility of a community of interest between the Soviet Union and the United States, but no expectation of a 'new civilization'. The last flicker of the dream faded as the tanks rumbled into Budapest to quell a workers' revolt.

It is not that we are short of problems. Any edition of any daily newspaper can provide us with a well assorted dozen. But the response is tired and dutiful, not urgent and zealous. The awakened are dozing, and soon may sleep again. They look to the future, but they look only for a modification and embellishment of the present, not for a new departure. The critics prod and satirize and find themselves fashionable, but they are ineffective unless they have awakeners to stimulate. There are not enough awakeners, and there is the cause of our accidie. We have so levelled that the supply of conscience-stricken social superiors is almost exhausted. We have moved so far from the original fount of social zeal that the impulse of religious fervour has faded, and there is no staying power in secular humanitarianism. There is no thrill of adventure in a programme which consists in adding a little bit more of what we have tried already, no progress in polishing the brasswork of a becalmed ship. We need again the wind of God to send us on our way.

I believe the wind is blowing. From the slight eminence to which we have so painfully attained it parts the mists and reveals in the distance new heights to be conquered. We are living in a Welfare State set in the midst of a desperately poor world. A hundred and fifty years of struggle in our own land against poverty, hunger, ignorance, and disease, may in the providence of God be a pilot scheme for a greater struggle on behalf of all the human race. Inextricably linked with the wider task is the challenge to abolish war and the warning that there is no unlimited time to meet it leisurely.

The awareness of the need, the realization of its critical urgency, and the coming of the skills and resources to meet it, have coincided in time. Our time. The gates of Hell will not be stormed and the Kingdom of God established on earth when all men have a reasonable expectation of an annual income of two hundred dollars. It is not the word of God for all time, nor all his word for this time, but it is surely part of what he is saying to his world and his Church from the midst of the turmoil of events; a light shining on the path to the next stage of our social pilgrimage.

FOR FURTHER READING

The Challenge of Hunger, Noel Drogat (Newman)
Common Sense About A Starving World, Ritchie Calder (Macmillan)
Aid For Developing Countries, H. J. P. Arnold (Dufour)
World Without Want, Paul G. Hoffman (Harper and Row)
Our Crowded Planet, ed. Fairfield Osborn (Doubleday)
Population and Society, Dennis Wrong (Random House)
The Race To The Year 2000, Fritz Baade (Doubleday)
The Stages of Economic Growth, W. W. Rostow (Cambridge)
Man In Rapid Social Change, Egbert de Vries (Doubleday)
American Capitalism, J. K. Galbraith (Houghton Mifflin)
Advertising, Walter Taplin (Little, Brown)
The Techniques of Persuasion, J. A. C. Brown (Pelican)
God and the Rich Society, D. L. Munby (Oxford)

INDEX